Great Danes

D1522911

Great Danes

The Complete Owner's Guide

Feeding, Housing, Training, Grooming,
and Breeding All Included.

Foreword

The Great Dane is a very large breed of dog, but that simply means that there is more of it to love. This giant breed is loyal and affectionate by nature, making it a loving companion and excellent family pet. Within the pages of this book you will receive a wealth of knowledge about the Great Dane breed including its characteristics, history, and care requirements. By the time you finish this book not only will you be properly equipped to decide whether the Great Dane is the right breed for you, but you will also be well on your way to becoming the best dog owner you can be.

Table of Contents

Chapter One: Introduction

The Great Dane is a very large dog breed of German descent that is also sometimes referred to as the German Mastiff. These dogs are one of the tallest dog breeds in the world with the world record holder being a Great Dane named Zeus who stood 44 inches (112cm) tall. Great Danes may be large but they are incredibly friendly and they can be very affectionate with family. These dogs are also surprisingly gentle with children, though their size can be problematic with very young children.

Great Danes are a unique and wonderful breed for a variety of different reasons which you will learn about in this book. Within the pages of this book you will receive a wealth of knowledge about the Great Dane breed including its characteristics, history, and care requirements.

Glossary of Terms

AKC – American Kennel Club, the largest purebred dog registry in the United States

Almond Eye – Referring to an elongated eye shape rather than a rounded shape

Apple Head – A round-shaped skull

Balance – A show term referring to all of the parts of the dog, both moving and standing, which produce a harmonious image

Beard – Long, thick hair on the dog's underjaw

Best in Show – An award given to the only undefeated dog left standing at the end of judging

Bitch – A female dog

Bite – The position of the upper and lower teeth when the dog's jaws are closed; positions include level, undershot, scissors, or overshot

Blaze – A white stripe running down the center of the face between the eyes

Blenheim – Refers to the red and white color of markings on the Cavalier King Charles Spaniel

Board – To house, feed, and care for a dog for a fee

Breed – A domestic race of dogs having a common gene pool and characterized appearance/function

Breed Standard – A published document describing the look, movement, and behavior of the perfect specimen of a particular breed

Buff – An off-white to gold coloring

Clip – A method of trimming the coat in some breeds

Coat – The hair covering of a dog; some breeds have two coats, and outer coat and undercoat; also known as a double coat. Examples of breeds with double coats include German Shepherd, Siberian Husky, Akita, etc.

Condition – The health of the dog as shown by its skin, coat, behavior, and general appearance

Crate – A container used to house and transport dogs; also called a cage or kennel

Crossbreed (Hybrid) – A dog having a sire and dam of two different breeds; cannot be registered with the AKC

Dam (bitch) – The female parent of a dog;

Dock – To shorten the tail of a dog by surgically removing the end part of the tail.

Double Coat – Having an outer weather-resistant coat and a soft, waterproof coat for warmth; see above.

Drop Ear – An ear in which the tip of the ear folds over and hangs down; not prick or erect

Entropion – A genetic disorder resulting in the upper or lower eyelid turning in

Fancier – A person who is especially interested in a particular breed or dog sport

Fawn – A red-yellow hue of brown

Feathering – A long fringe of hair on the ears, tail, legs, or body of a dog

Groom – To brush, trim, comb or otherwise make a dog's coat neat in appearance

Heel – To command a dog to stay close by its owner's side

Hip Dysplasia – A condition characterized by the abnormal formation of the hip joint

Inbreeding – The breeding of two closely related dogs of one breed

Kennel – A building or enclosure where dogs are kept

Litter – A group of puppies born at one time

Markings – A contrasting color or pattern on a dog's coat

Mask – Dark shading on the dog's foreface

Mate – To breed a dog and a bitch

Neuter – To castrate a male dog or spay a female dog

Pads – The tough, shock-absorbent skin on the bottom of a dog's foot

Parti-Color – A coloration of a dog's coat consisting of two or more definite, well-broken colors; one of the colors must be white

Pedigree – The written record of a dog's genealogy going back three generations or more

Pied – A coloration on a dog consisting of patches of white and another color

Prick Ear – Ear that is carried erect, usually pointed at the tip of the ear

Puppy – A dog under 12 months of age

Purebred – A dog whose sire and dam belong to the same breed and who are of unmixed descent

Saddle – Colored markings in the shape of a saddle over the back; colors may vary

Self Color – Having one color or whole color except for light-colored shading

Shedding – The natural process whereby old hair falls off the dog's body as it is replaced by new hair growth.

Sire – The male parent of a dog

Smooth Coat – Short hair that is close-lying

Spay – The surgery to remove a female dog's ovaries, rendering her incapable of breeding

Trim – To groom a dog's coat by plucking or clipping

Undercoat – The soft, short coat typically concealed by a longer outer coat

Wean – The process through which puppies transition from subsisting on their mother's milk to eating solid food

Whelping – The act of birthing a litter of puppies

Chapter Two: Understanding Great Danes

Before you decide whether or not the Great Dane is the right breed for you and your family, you need to take the time to learn as much as you can about it. The Great Dane is a large dog that requires a certain degree of care – if you cannot provide for its needs, you should consider a different breed or another pet entirely. In this chapter you will learn the basics about Great Danes including general facts, the breed history, and types of Great Dane. This information should be enough to get you started in making up your mind about this wonderful breed.

1.) What are Great Danes?

The American Kennel Club (AKC) describes the Great Dane as a "friendly, patient, dependable" breed. This dog is a large, regal-looking breed and it is ranked as the 15th most popular breed in the United States according to AKC registration statistics. Great Danes are more than just big dogs – they are also loyal and loving companions. These dogs are not overly active and they are generally healthy – all of these characteristics combine to make the Great Dane a great choice for dog lovers.

The Great Dane is known for its great height and muscular build, but it is also known for being affectionate and loving with family. This breed may look intimidating due to its size, but it has a soft heart and a friendly temperament. For the most part, this breed gets along well with strangers and other dogs, plus they can be very gentle around children as well. Of course, you need to supervise the Great Dane around children because, while the dog is unlikely to be aggressive, its large size means that he may accidentally knock a child over.

Great Danes are unique from other breeds primarily due to their size. The giant size of this breed has a significant impact on its development and maturity – this breed is likely to exhibit puppy-like characteristics for at least two years or more. This being the case, caring for a Great Dane puppy can be a challenge, especially for new dog owners. If you are looking for a smart and friendly breed that will give you an endless supply of unconditional love, however, the Great Dane is a great breed worthy of your consideration.

2.) Facts About Great Danes

The Great Dane is a very large German breed, sometimes referred to as the German mastiff. This breed holds the world record for being the tallest dog, measured at 44 inches (112 cm) from paw to shoulder. Great Danes were developed as hunting dogs, bred to hunt large prey like boar and deer, though they were also kept as companion pets by members of German nobility. To this day, the Great Dane is a popular companion pet.

The AKC describes the Great Dane as a combination of "regal appearance, dignity, strength, and elegance with great size and a powerful, well-formed, smoothly muscled body". In essence, the Great Dane is a big, muscular dog.

For as large as the Great Dane is, however, its long legs do not give it an air of awkwardness. The Great Dane carries himself with refinement and he has a well-balanced appearance with a graceful mobility.

Great Danes have a somewhat square build and males of the breed are typically larger and more muscular than females. The average male Great Dane stands at least 30 inches (76 cm) tall at the shoulders and a female stands at least 28 inches (71 cm) tall. In terms of weight, male Great Danes generally weigh about 120 pounds (54 kg) at the 18-month mark while females weigh closer to 100 pounds (45 kg). A fully grown Great Dane, however, might weigh anywhere between 120 and 200 pounds (54 to 90 kg), depending on sex and breeding.

Size is not the only thing that sets the Great Dane apart from other breeds. This dog also has a massive head that is long and narrow. The neck is graceful and long, leading down to muscular shoulders. Great Danes have very large, triangular ears that are naturally floppy. In some areas, however, the ears are likely to be cropped, making them pointed and erect. The Great Dane has dark, deep-set eyes and a large nose that matches the coat color – usually black or blue/black. The tail of this breed is naturally long and tapered to a point, carried high.

The Great Dane has a short, dense coat that is easy to groom but it still sheds a lot. In terms of coat color, there are three color varieties that make up a total of six different coat colors. The three color varieties are fawn and brindle; harlequin and black; and blue. Within the fawn and brindle color variety there are two options – a yellow-gold coat color with black mask or a yellow-gold coat color with a chevron stripe pattern. Within the harlequin and black color variety there are three color options – solid black, white with irregular black patches, or mantle (black and white with solid black blanket over the body). The final color variety is pure steel blue.

In terms of temperament, the Great Dane is very friendly and he tends to get along well with everyone he meets. This breed often views itself as a lap dog, though it is clearly too large to actually be one, and it constantly seeks affection from its owners. Great Danes generally get along well with other dogs and non-canine pets, plus they do not have a very high prey drive. This breed is gentle around children, though supervision is recommended simply due to the size of the dog. This breed responds well to training but it does require a great deal of socialization from an early age.

As you might expect from a giant breed, the Great Dane is fairly short-lived – the average lifespan for the breed is 7 to 10 years. Despite its short lifespan, the Great

Dane is still a fairly healthy breed. Like all dogs, however, the Great Dane is prone to developing certain health problems. Some of the conditions most likely to affect this breed include hip dysplasia, gastric torsion, bone cancer, and heart disease. These dogs are also at risk for developmental problems, so feeding a proper diet is essential for the healthy development of this breed.

Summary of Great Dane Facts

Pedigree: bred from large boarhounds originating in Greece, developed in Germany during the 16th century, possibly crossed with English Mastiff and Irish Wolfhound

Breed Size: giant

Height (male): minimum 30 inches (76 cm)

Height (female): minimum 28 inches (71 cm)

Weight (male): minimum 120 lbs. (54 kg)

Weight (female): minimum 100 lbs. (45 kg)

Coat Length: short and close-lying

Coat Texture: smooth and dense

Color: fawn, brindle, blue, black, harlequin, and mantle

Markings: depends on color; may exhibit black mask, tiger-stripe pattern, black patches, or a solid black blanket

Eyes and Nose: dark, matches coat color

Ears: large and triangular, naturally floppy but sometimes cropped to a point

Tail: long and tapered to a point, carried high

Temperament: moderate energy, friendly, affectionate with family, gentle, not aggressive

Training: intelligent and eager to please, easy to housetrain

Exercise Needs: moderately high; 30 minute daily walk is generally sufficient

Lifespan: average 7 to 10 years

Health Conditions: hip dysplasia, gastric torsion, bone cancer, heart disease, developmental issues

3.) Great Dane Breed History

The exact origins of the Great Dane are unknown because there are several similar-looking breeds that have been identified throughout history. Perhaps the oldest Great Dane-like breed dates back to drawings on ancient Egyptian artifacts from 3,000 BC – similar drawings were also found in Babylonian temples dating back to 2,000 BC. Another report suggests that a breed similar to the Great Dane originated in Tibet around 1121 BC.

Although the exact origins of this breed are unknown, it is a common theory that early Great Danes were transported to various parts of the world by the

Assyrians. It is hypothesized that the Assyrians traded the dogs to the ancient Romans and Greeks who then crossed the dogs with other breed including ancestors of the English Mastiff and the Irish Wolfhound. The dogs resulting from these crosses were referred to as Boar Hounds because they were used to hunt boar.

During the 16th century, Boar Hounds were subjected to a name change and started to become known as English Dogges. Later in that same century, however, the breed became popular among German nobility and they came to be known as Kammerhunde, or chamber dogs. It wasn't until the 1700s that the name Great Dane came into use. This occurred when a French naturalist saw a slim, Greyhound-like specimen of the Boar Hound breed. He named the dog Grand Danois which eventually became Great Danish Dog. This new name for the breed stuck, even though the breed was not developed in Denmark.

In 1880, a group of dog breeders and judges gathered to discuss the Great Danish Dog breed. They decided that since the breed was distinct from the English Mastiff that it deserved a name of its own – thus the breed came to be known as the Deutsche Dogge, or German Dog. This same group founded the Deutscher Doggen-Klub of Germany and before long, several other European countries had adopted the name. The group continued to refine the breed throughout the late 1800s and they began to turn their attention to the breed's temperament.

During the early years of development, aggressive and ferocious temperaments were favored because the Great Dane was used to hunt wild boar. As the breed became more popular among German nobility, however, a milder temperament was called for. Breeder were successful in producing a gentler temperament and the modern Great Dane is still very friendly. It is unknown when the breed came to the United States, but the Great Dane Club of America was founded in 1889 and the AKC recognized the Great Dane in 1887.

4.) Types of Great Danes

There is technically only one breed of Great Dane, though there are six different colors recognized by the AKC breed standard. <u>These six colors are described below</u>:

Fawn – A yellow-gold color over the entire body with a black mask on the eye rims and eyebrows.

Brindle – A yellow-gold cover over the entire body with a black chevron stripe pattern.

Black – A solid glossy black color. Any white markings on the chest or toes are considered faults.

Harlequin – A base color of pure white with torn black patches distributed irregularly over the whole body.

Mantle – A black-and-white coloration with a solid black blanket over the whole body. A black skull with a white muzzle is preferred, a white blaze is optional.

Blue – Pure steel blue color over the entire body. Any white markings on the chest or toes are considered faults.

Chapter Three: What to Know Before Buying

In reading the previous chapter you received a wealth of knowledge about the Great Dane breed in general. In this chapter you will learn the specifics about keeping this breed – this information will be instrumental in helping you decide whether the Great Dane is the right breed for you. In this chapter you will find information about licensing your dog, keeping your dog with other pets, and even the pros and cons for the breed. You will also receive detailed information about the costs associated with keeping a Great Dane so you can make sure you are able to care for a dog financially before you buy one.

1.) Do You Need a License?

Before you bring home a new pet, you need to make sure that it is legal in your area to do so. Certain states, provinces, and countries have laws against keeping certain kinds of pets so you want to check out your local licensing requirements just to be safe. In the United States, there are no federal rules requiring dog owners to license their dogs. There are, however, licensing requirements at the state level. It is mandatory in most states for dog owners to license their dogs, so check with your local council to see what the rules are for your state.

In order to obtain a license for your dog in the United States you will have to fill out an application and submit proof of a current rabies vaccination. In the United States, dog licenses cost about $25 (£22.50) and they must be renewed each year. In order to renew your dog license you will also have to renew your dog's rabies vaccination. You can talk to your veterinarian or contact your local council for specific details about licensing your dog. For more information about licensing requirements in the United States, visit the following website:

<https://www.aphis.usda.gov/animal_welfare/
downloads/aw/awlicreg.pdf>

In the United Kingdom, licensing requirements are a little bit different. It is mandatory throughout the U.K. for dog owners to license their dogs and these licenses are renewable annually. The only exception is for puppies under 6 months of age and for police dogs or assistance dogs. Another difference is that you do not need to have a rabies vaccination in order to get your dog licensed in the U.K. because rabies has been eradicated. For more information about licensing requirements in the United Kingdom, visit the following website:

<http://www.nidirect.gov.uk/dog-licensing>

2.) How Many Great Danes Should You Keep?

The answer to this question is not a simple Yes or No because there are many factors to take into consideration. First, you need to make sure that you can provide for a single Great Dane before you even think about getting two of them. Due to their size, Great Danes require a lot of indoor space so you shouldn't get even on Great Dane if you live in a small condo or apartment. Great Danes do not necessarily need a lot of exercise, but they do need plenty of indoor space.

Another important factor to consider when thinking about keeping more than one Great Dane is the cost. Great Dane puppies go for prices as high as $3,000 for show-quality purebreds, so the cost to purchase more than one may be prohibitive. You then need to factor in the cost of feeding both dogs as well as veterinary costs. These costs add up very quickly and, unless you are able to cover all of the financial requirements for being a Great Dane owner, you shouldn't bring home a puppy.

If you are simply thinking in practical terms, having a second dog around to keep your Great Dane company may not be a bad idea. These dogs are very friendly by nature and they get along well with other dogs when properly socialized. Great Danes also require a great deal of attention from family so, if you work a full-time job, having a second dog around might be beneficial for your Great Dane. You do not necessarily have to purchase two Great Danes, but having a second dog would not be a bad thing.

3.) Do Great Danes Get Along with Other Pets?

As you have already learned, the Great Dane is a gentle and affectionate breed with family. Even though this breed was originally developed to hunt boar, selective breeding processes were successful in breeding out the aggression and ferocious nature for which early Great Danes were known. The modern Great Dane get along well with people and animals alike.

The Great Dane typically gets along very well with other dogs, though you might want to be careful about keeping a very small dog with a Great Dane because accidents may happen due to the Great Dane's size. These dogs were bred for hunting, but they have a fairly low prey drive which means that they are unlikely to bother non-canine pets. Your best bet to make sure that your Great Dane gets along with other household pets is to raise them together from a young age.

4.) Ease and Cost of Care

Owning and caring for a dog is not cheap, especially if it is a giant breed like the Great Dane. Before you decide whether or not this is the right breed for you, you need to make sure that you can cover the costs to keep a dog like the Great Dane. In this section you will find an overview of the costs associated with Great Dane ownership including initial costs and monthly costs.

a.) Initial Costs

The initial costs of Great Dane ownership include the cost of the dog itself as well as necessary supplies and equipment to get started. This may include your dog's crate, a dog bed, food and water bowls, toys, and other accessories. You will also have to have your dog vaccinated and you should have him microchipped as well. You also need to have your puppy spayed or neutered if you do not plan to breed him or her. <u>You will find an overview of these costs below as well as an estimate for each</u>:

Purchase Price – The cost to purchase a Great Dane puppy will vary greatly depending on several factors. First of all, a purebred Great Dane will be more expensive than a mixed breed and a show-quality puppy will be the most expensive of all. You should plan to spend between $600 and $2,500 (£540 - £2,250) on your Great Dane puppy.

Crate – Having a crate for your puppy is very important because it will give him a place to sleep and it is essential for housetraining. You should purchase a crate that is just large enough for your puppy to comfortably stand up, turn around, and lie down in – this may mean purchasing an upgrade as your puppy grows. You should plan to spend about $35 (£31.50) for your puppy's first crate.

Dog Bed – To make your puppy's crate more comfortable you should line it with a plush dog bed. If you are worried about your puppy having accidents you can start with some old towels or an old blanket until your puppy is housetrained, then you can switch to a dog bed. You should plan to spend about $20 (£18) on a plain dog bed.

Food/Water Bowls – You can find cheap food and water bowls at any pet store, but you would be better off buying a high-quality set at the beginning. Stainless steel food bowls are not very expensive and they are easy to clean, plus they won't harbor bacteria like plastic bowls can. Ceramic bowls are another good option. You should plan to spend between $15 and $30 (£13.50 - £27) on a set of bowls.

Toys and Accessories – In addition to purchasing a set of food and water bowls, you also need to provide your new puppy with plenty of toys. You will also need a collar and leash, plus a harness for training. The cost for these items will vary depending on quality but you should budget about $100 (£90) to be safe.

Vaccinations – While your Great Dane puppy is less than a year old he will need to get certain vaccinations every few weeks. Depending how old your puppy is when you bring him home, the breeder may have already given him some vaccines. Talk to your veterinarian about your puppy's vaccination schedule and be prepared to spend up to $100 (£90) for initial vaccinations.

Microchipping – Having your dog microchipped is a great idea, even if your dog will be carrying and ID tag on his collar. If your dog gets lost, whoever finds him will be able to take him to a local shelter to have his microchip scanned. Each microchip is linked to a number which is correlated to the owner's contact information. The microchip will be implanted under your dog's skin in a procedure that only takes a few minutes to complete and costs about $30 (£27).

Spay/Neuter Surgery – Unless you plan to breed your Great Dane (a decision that should not be made lightly), you should have your puppy spayed or neutered before 6 months of age. The cost of this procedure will vary depending on whether you have it done by a veterinary surgeon or if you take your puppy to a vet clinic. If you go to a clinic, you might pay as little as $50 (£45) for neuter surgery and about $100 (£90) for spay surgery.

Initial Costs for Great Danes		
Cost	**One Dog**	**Two Dogs**
Purchase Price	$600 to $2,500 (£540 - £2,250)	$1,200 to $5,000 (£1,080 - £4,500)
Crate	$35 (£31.50)	$70 (£63)
Dog Bed	$20 (£18)	$40 (£36)
Food/Water Bowls	$15 to $30 (£13.50 - £27)	$30 to $60 (£27 - £54)
Toys/Accessories	$100 (£90)	$200 (£180)
Vaccinations	$100 (£90)	$200 (£180)

Microchipping	$30 (£27)	$60 (£54)
Spay/Neuter	$50 to $100 (£45 to £90)	$100 to $200 (£90 to £180)
Total	$950 to $2,915 (£855 - £2,624)	$1,900 to $5,830 (£1,710 - £5,247)

*These rates are based on a conversion rate of $1 U.S. to £0.90 U.K. Rates are subject to change.

b.) Monthly Costs

The monthly costs associated with owning a Great Dane include certain costs that recur on a monthly basis. The most important of these costs is food. Other monthly costs include flea/tick prevention, heartworm medication, veterinary care, grooming costs and license renewal. You will find an overview of these costs below as well as an estimate for each:

Food and Treats – The biggest monthly expense you will have to cover for your Great Dane is food and treats. Because the Great Dane is such a large breed he may eat as much as 7 to 10 cups of dry food per day. In order to keep your Great Dane healthy you should choose a high-quality food made with premium ingredients – this will not come cheap. You should budget about $60 to $100 (£54 - £90) per month for food and add an extra $10 (£9) per month for your dog's treats.

Flea/Tick Prevention – Another important monthly cost is flea/tick prevention. This is very important because ticks can carry dangerous diseases and fleas can cause allergic reactions. Plus, it is difficult to get a flea infestation under control. You should plan to spend about $20 (£18) per month on a high-quality flea and tick preventive.

Heartworm Medication – In addition to flea and tick prevention, you also need to give your dog heartworm medication on a monthly basis. This will cost about $10 (£9) per month.

Veterinary Care – To keep your Great Dane in good health you should take him to the vet for a check-up every six months. The cost for a typical vet visit may vary from one office to another, but you should plan to spend between $50 and $75 on a vet visit. Two visits per year divided over twelve months' averages to about $12.50 (£11) per month.

Grooming – Great Danes have short coats but they are fairly dense which means that they shed fairly heavily. You should plan to brush your Great Dane several times a week and you might want to have him professionally groomed about twice per year. The average cost to groom a Great Dane is between $50 and $100. Two trips to the groomer over twelve months averages to about $8 to $16 (£7 - £14.50) per month.

License Renewal – You will need to renew your dog's license annually and it only costs about $25 (£22.50). If you divide that cost over 12 months it averages to about $2 (£1.80) per month.

Other Costs – In addition to the costs already discussed you should be prepared to cover some unexpected costs just in case. These may include the cost to replace damaged toys, larger collars as your puppy grows, and things like ear cleaner solution and dog toothpaste. You should budget for about $15 (£13.50) per month for these additional costs.

Monthly Costs for Great Danes		
Cost	**One Dog**	**Two Dogs**
Food and Treats	$70 to $110 (£63 - £99)	$140 to $220 (£126 - £198)
Flea/Tick Meds	$20 (£18)	$40 (£36)
Heartworm Meds	$10 (£9)	$20 (£18)
Veterinary Care	$12.50 (£11)	$24 (£21)

Grooming	$8 to $16 (£7 - £14.50)	$16 to $32 (£14.50 - £29)
License Renewal	$2 (£1.80)	$4 (£3.60)
Other Costs	$15 (£13.50)	$30 (£27)
Total	$138 to $186 (£124 - £167)	$274 to $370 (£247 - £333)

*These rates are based on a conversion rate of $1 U.S. to £0.90 U.K. Rates are subject to change.

5.) Pros and Cons for Great Danes

The Great Dane is a wonderful breed, but it is not the right choice for everyone. Before you decide whether or not to purchase a Great Dane, take the time to learn the pros and cons of the breed.

Pros for Great Danes

- Very friendly and gentle breed; makes a great companion pet.
- Unique and beautiful appearance; comes in six different color varieties.
- Gets along well with other dogs and non-canine pets; low prey drive.
- Typically gentle around children but should be supervised due to size.
- Short coat is very easy to groom, though frequent brushing is recommended to control shedding.

Cons for Great Danes

- Very large breed; needs a great deal of space, not recommended for condos or apartments.

- Requires a great deal of socialization from a young age to ensure a friendly and even temperament.
- Needs a great deal of time and attention, especially during the puppy stage.
- Short coat is not designed for cold weather – should be an indoor dog only.
- Very short-lived breed, average lifespan is only 7 to 10 years.
- Prone to several health problems including hip dysplasia, gastric torsion, heart problems, and developmental issues.
- Purchase price is very high and the cost to feed a Great Dane is lofty as well.

Chapter Four: Purchasing a Great Dane

After reading the information in the previous chapter, you should have a good understanding of the Great Dane breed and you may be ready to decide whether or not it is the right dog for you. If it is, this chapter will help you learn where to look for Great Dane breeders and how to choose a healthy puppy from a litter. Choosing a healthy puppy is important because it sets your dog up for a long, healthy life. In this chapter you will also receive tips for puppy-proofing your home and for introducing your new Great Dane puppy to family.

1.) Where to Buy a Great Dane

If you are ready to purchase a Great Dane, your first instinct might be to head to your local pet store. If you speak to experienced dog owners, however, many of them will caution you against this. While some pet stores get their dogs from local rescues or reputable breeders, many of them get their puppies from puppy mills. A puppy mill is a breeding operation that subjects dogs to horrible conditions, forcing them to produce litter after litter of puppies until they are physically incapable of doing so. The puppies that result from this kind of breeding are often prone to genetic diseases as well as malnutrition, poor socialization, and poor breeding in general. Before you buy a Great Dane puppy from the pet store, take the time to consider your other options.

a.) Buying a Puppy

If you are absolutely certain you want a Great Dane puppy, your best bet is to find a reputable breeder. You may be able to get information about breeders at your local pet store, even if you choose not to buy your puppy there. Other places you can look for breeder information include your vet's office and online. If you want to make sure that your Great Dane puppy is healthy, take the time to find a reputable breeder who follows responsible breeding practices. You will find more information about selecting a breeder in the next section.

b. Adopting a Rescue Dog

If you aren't concerned with getting a puppy, you may want to consider adopting a Great Dane from a local rescue operation. When you adopt a dog from a shelter you could be literally saving a life because some shelters are forced to euthanize animals that do not get adopted simply because they don't have enough space to accommodate all of them. Even so-called "no-kill" shelters are sometimes forced to euthanize animals if they do not have a good chance of being adopted.

Adopting a rescue dog has many advantages over purchasing a puppy. For one thing, the cost to adopt a dog is generally under $150 (£135) whereas a Great Dane puppy purchased from a breeder could cost three times that much. Another benefit of adopting a rescue dog is that it will already likely be spayed or neutered and up to date on vaccinations. Depending on the age of the dog, he may also have some obedience training under his belt.

If you are considering adopting a Great Dane, consider one of the following rescues or shelters:

United States Great Dane Rescues:

Great Dane Rescue.

<http://www.greatdanerescueinc.com/>

Pennsylvania Great Dane Rescue.

<http://www.pennsylvania-dane-rescue.org/>

Mid-Atlantic Great Dane Rescue League, Inc.

<http://www.magdrl.org/>

Harlequin Haven Great Dane Rescue.

<http://www.ohiodanerescue.com/>

Forever Friends Great Dane Rescue.

<http://www.foreverfriendsgdri.com/>

United Kingdom Great Dane Rescues:

The Kennel Club Great Dane Breed Rescue List.

<http://www.thekennelclub.org.uk/services/public/findares
cue/Default.aspx?breed=5124>

Great Dane Adoption Society.

<http://www.danes.org.uk/>

Daneline International Charitable Foundation.

<http://www.daneline.co.uk/>

Great Dane Adoption Society.

<http://www.supportadoptionforpets.co.uk/rescue-
centres/great-dane-adoption-society/great-dane-adoption-
society>

Great Dane Rescue UK.

<http://www.greatdanerescue.co.uk/>

2.) *Choosing a Reputable Breeder*

A responsible dog breeder will be more concerned about finding a good home for his puppies than he will be about making money. Reputable breeders are in it to preserve and better the breed – they aren't in it for the money. If you really want to make sure that the Great Dane you bring home is in good health and has been bred properly, you need to take the time to do your research and to find a reputable breeder.

To start your search you can contact your local vet's office or pet store – you can also ask around for recommendations from friends and family who own dogs. If none of these options work, you can perform an internet search to find local breeders in your area. No matter how you find the breeders, make sure you put together a list of several options and then go through the list to find the best breeder available. <u>After gathering your list of breeders, follow the steps below to make your choice</u>:

1. View each breeder's website, if they have one, and look for key things like information about the breeder's experience, a license from the AKC or Kennel Club, and photos of the breeding facilities.

2. Contact each breeder by phone and ask them questions about their experience with breeding dogs in general and with the Great Dane breed in particular.

3. Remove any breeders from the list who refuse to answer your questions and those who do not seem to be knowledgeable about the breed.

4. Look for breeders that show an interest in learning more about you – reputable breeders want to make sure their puppies go to good homes so they will probably ask you questions as well.

5. Narrow down your list of breeders to about three options based on their answers to your questions.

6. Visit each breeder's location to get a feel for the operation – ask for a tour of the facilities and make sure you see the breeding stock as well as the puppies.

7. Cross any breeder off your list if they do not agree to show you the facilities or if they seem to be in disrepair – you also want to avoid breeders who won't show you the breeding stock or if the dogs do not

appear to be in good health.

8. Ask to see the puppies that are available and make sure they are kept in clean conditions – any signs of diarrhea, dirty bedding, or other signs of uncleanliness are a red flag.

9. Select the breeder that you feel is the most knowledgeable and experienced with Great Danes – be sure to ask about what comes with the puppy when you purchase (you should get a pedigree as well as health records for the puppy you buy).

10. Go through the process of reserving a puppy if they are not ready to come home yet – you will probably be asked to put down a deposit.

Now that you know how to select a reputable breeder, you are ready to learn how to pick out a healthy puppy from a litter.

3.) Selecting a Healthy Great Dane Puppy

Once you've taken the time to vet your Great Dane breeder you then need to actually select your puppy. It is essential that you take the time to choose your puppy carefully because you want to make sure that it is in good health when you bring it home. Do not give in to the temptation to "rescue" an unhealthy puppy because it will only set you up for heartbreak. The puppy will likely decline in health and you'll find yourself saddled with expensive vet bills – the puppy might even die within weeks of you bringing it home.

<u>Follow the steps below to select a healthy Great Dane puppy from a litter:</u>

1. Take a moment to observe the litter as a whole – the puppies should be active and playing with each other, not lazing around.

2. Gauge the response of the puppies to your presence – they should be curious, not frightened.

3. Approach the puppies and give them time to get used to you – they should show a healthy curiosity and eagerness to interact with you.

4. Spend a few minutes interacting with the puppies as a group, playing with them and watching how they interact with each other.

5. Pick out a puppy one-by-one and spend some time with each one to get a feel for their temperaments.

6. Check the puppies for obvious signs of illness – this includes things like nasal discharge, watery eyes, difficulty breathing, signs of diarrhea, lethargic behavior, uneven coat, bumps or sores, and vision

problems.

7. Handle each of the puppies to see how they respond to human touch – you can try picking them up and cradling them in your arms.

8. Choose the puppy that you feel is the best match for you and your family based on temperament – keep in mind that temperament is malleable, so you will still need to train and socialize the puppy.

After you have taken the time to view all of the puppies and you've made your choice, talk to the breeder about the process of reserving a puppy. If the puppies have already been weaned, you may be able to take your puppy home right away. If not, you'll probably have to put down a deposit and come back later.

4.) Puppy-Proofing Your Home

Once you've chosen your puppy, your next task is to prepare your home. Puppies are naturally curious and they do not know when something is potentially dangerous. It is your job as a dog owner to prepare your home to ensure the safety of your puppy – this is called puppy-proofing. Follow the steps below to puppy-proof your home:

1. Make sure all food items are stored in closed-lid containers and put away.

2. Store all of your cleaning products and chemicals in a cabinet or storage bin that your puppy can't access.

3. Make sure all of your medications and toiletry items are stored in the medicine cabinet or placed out of your puppy's reach.

4. Keep a lid on your trashcan and recycling containers so your puppy can't get into them.

5. Check the list of toxic plants provided later in this book to make sure none of your houseplants are harmful for dogs – if they are, remove them from the

home or put them out of your puppy's reach.

6. Tie up any loose cords or electric cables so your puppy won't be tempted to chew on them.

7. Cover any open bodies of water (this includes the toilet) that could be a drowning risk for your puppy.

8. Use plastic covers to plug all of the unused outlets in your home so your puppy doesn't electrocute himself.

9. Keep all small objects and toys off the ground – make sure your children know to clean up after themselves.

10. Make sure your yard is properly fenced for your puppy's safety, if you have an outdoor space.

11. Avoid using tobacco products in the house and make sure to dispose of cigarette butts properly.

In addition to following these puppy-proofing steps also need to supervise your puppy when he is not in his crate to make sure he doesn't get into trouble.

5.) Introducing Your Puppy to Children

If you have children, you need to be careful about how you introduce them to your puppy. Children can be very excited about a new puppy and they could accidentally hurt the puppy if they are not careful. Your children could also do something that scares the puppy, causing him to react by nipping or biting. <u>For the safety of your puppy and your children, follow the steps below to properly introduce the two</u>:

1. Talk to your children before you even bring the puppy home about how to properly handle it – make sure they know to be gentle and quiet.

2. Make sure your children know that the puppy might be nervous when you first bring him home, so they shouldn't expect him to be playful right away.

3. When you are ready to make introductions, have your children sit quietly on the floor and bring the puppy to them.

4. Place your puppy on the floor with your children but let him make the decision to approach them – do not

let your children chase the puppy around or grab him.

5. When the puppy feels comfortable enough to approach your children, instruct them to pet him gently on the head and back.

6. Allow your children to offer the puppy a few small treats to encourage him to approach them.

7. Give your children time to play with the puppy but make sure to keep an eye on his reaction – if the puppy seems to get tired or overwhelmed, cut the session short.

8. If your children are old enough to do so safely, allow them to carefully pick the puppy up and hold him in their laps.

Supervise the entire interaction between your children and your puppy and cut it off if the puppy seems overwhelmed. It will take time for the puppy to get used to his new surroundings and to get used to being handled by your children. Just make sure that your children are patient and keep the introduction sessions short so the puppy doesn't become overwhelmed.

Chapter Five: Caring for Great Danes

When you bring your Great Dane home, you want him to feel as comfortable as possible. The best way to do this is to make sure that he has some space of his own where he can retreat to if he needs a break from people. In this chapter you will learn about your Great Dane's habitat and exercise requirements. You will also receive tips for purchasing the right supplies and equipment for your dog as well as information about setting up that special area for your Great Dane.

1.) Habitat and Exercise Requirements

The Great Dane is a giant breed, so it requires a good deal of indoor space. This being the case, a Great Dane is probably not the right choice for you if you live in a small condo or apartment. Great Danes are not an overly active breed so you don't necessarily have to have a great deal of outdoor space for him to run and play, but you do need to make sure he gets adequate daily exercise. Avoid strenuous activity like running, however, because it could put excess strain on your Great Dane's bones and joints, putting him at an increased risk for musculoskeletal disorders.

It is also important to note that the Great Dane is not an outdoor breed – it does not have a thick, double coat to protect him from extreme weather. Unless you are able to keep your Great Dane comfortably indoors, you should consider another breed. You should never keep your Great Dane outdoors for extended periods of time in cold weather and you need to be careful about leaving him outside when it is hot as well. Make sure your dog has access to plenty of shade and fresh water during the summer to avoid heat stroke or other complications.

2.) Necessary Supplies and Equipment

The Great Dane is not what most dog owners would consider a high-maintenance breed, but there are certain supplies and equipment you will need. These include:

- Food and water bowls
- Collar, leash and harness
- Crate or kennel
- Dog bed or blanket
- Assortment of toys
- Grooming supplies

Food and Water Bowls – You don't necessarily need to spend a lot on food and water bowls for your dog, but you should make sure that they are made from quality materials. Stainless steel is the best option because it is durable and resistant to bacteria.

Collar, Leash and Harness – It is essential that you have a collar for your Great Dane because it will carry your dog's license and ID tag. You will need to start with a small collar for your puppy and get larger collars as he grows – the same is true for his leash. In addition to a collar and leash, you should also consider a harness. Using a harness when you take your dog for a walk is a great option because it will prevent too much pressure from being placed on the dog's neck which could cause injury. A harness distributes the force from the leash across the chest and back which is much safer for the dog.

Crate or Kennel – To keep your dog confined when you are not at home or unable to watch him you will need a crate or kennel. Your dog's crate should be just large enough for him to comfortably stand up, turn around, and lie down in – if it is too much larger, it could increase the risk of your puppy having an accident. Because Great Danes grow so slowly you may need to start with a small crate for your puppy and buy progressively larger ones as he grows.

Dog Bed or Blanket – To make your dog's crate more comfortable you should line it with a plush dog bed or blanket. If you are worried about accidents while you are crate training your puppy, start with an old blanket or towel then switch to a dog bed once your puppy is trained.

Assortment of Toys – Having an assortment of toys around is essential for a number of reasons. For one thing, it will help to keep your dog from chewing on household objects, as long as you train him to only chew on his toys. Also, toys will help to keep your dog occupied when you aren't able to pay attention to him – this will reduce the risk for problem behaviors or destructive tendencies.

Grooming Supplies – To keep your Great Dane's coat healthy you should purchase a rubber curry comb for brushing as well as a pair of dog nail clippers. You'll also want to keep some dog-friendly shampoo on hand for when you need to bathe your Great Dane.

3.) Setting Up Your Great Dane's Crate

When you are not at home, or when you aren't able to directly supervise your Great Dane, you want to know that he will stay out of trouble. The best way to do this is to create a special area for your Great Dane to call his own using a puppy play pen – you can also use other means to fence off a section of the room where you plan to keep your dog's crate. Inside this area, place your dog's crate as well as his food and water bowls plus his toys. You will confine your puppy to the crate overnight and when you aren't home at least until he is housetrained. At that point you can then let him have free-reign of the enclosed area when you aren't able to supervise him directly.

Chapter Six: Feeding Your Great Dane

The quality of your Great Dane's diet will be directly reflected by his physical health and well-being. For this reason, it is essential that you choose a high-quality and nutritious diet for your dog. Unfortunately, there are so many options for dog food out there that it can be difficult to make a good choice. In this chapter you will learn the basics about your dog's nutritional requirements and you will receive tips for picking a commercial dog food that will meet those needs. You'll also find tips for avoiding toxic plants and food items for your dog.

1.) Nutritional Requirements for Dogs

If you want your Great Dane to live a long and healthy life, you absolutely must provide him with a nutritious diet. Dogs have different nutritional needs than humans, so you first need to learn about those requirements before you go shopping for dog food. While dogs are a carnivorous species, they do require some carbohydrates as well – their diet should not be entirely composed of meat. Below you will find an overview of the nutritional needs for dogs – the most important nutrients are: protein, fat, carbohydrate, vitamins and minerals.

Protein – Protein is the most important nutritional consideration for dogs because it plays a key role in the growth and development of tissues and organs. Protein is made up of amino acids, some of which your dog's body is capable of producing (these are called non-essential amino acids) and some of which must come from his diet (these are essential amino acids). Your dog should get the majority of his protein from animal sources like meat, fish, and eggs – plant-based sources of protein are less biologically valuable for dogs.

Fat – While too much fat in your Great Dane's diet could lead to obesity, he does need some fat. Fat is the most highly concentrated source of energy available to dogs and it should come from animal-based sources like chicken fat or salmon oil. Like proteins, plant-based fats are less biologically valuable to dogs than animal-based sources. Your dog should get a blend of omega-3 and omega-6 fatty acids to support his immune system and to promote skin and coat health.

Carbohydrates – Dogs do not have specific requirements for carbohydrate but these foods provide dietary fiber as well as various vitamins and minerals. Your dog should get his carbohydrate from high-quality, easily digestible sources like whole grains or fresh fruits and vegetables. Low-quality fillers like corn, wheat, and soy ingredients are best avoided because they don't offer much nutritional value for your dog.

Vitamins – A dog's body is not capable of producing most essential vitamins on its own, so they must come from his diet. The vitamins that are most important for dogs include vitamin A, vitamin D, vitamin E and vitamin C. These vitamins should come from whole food sources because they will be easier for your dog's body to absorb than if they came from supplements alone.

Minerals – Like vitamins, your dog's body is unable to synthesize most minerals so they must come from his diet. The most important minerals for dogs include calcium, phosphorus, potassium, sodium, copper, zinc, and iron. Your dog should get most of these minerals from whole food sources but there is a certain type of mineral supplement that is easy for your dog's body to absorb – chelated minerals. These are minerals that have been chemically bonded to protein molecules, making them easier to absorb and digest.

Water – The most important nutrient for any animal is water. Your dog needs constant access to fresh water at all times, so make sure he has several water bowls distributed around the house.

2.) *How to Choose a Healthy Dog Food*

Now that you understand the basics about your Great Dane's nutritional needs you will be better equipped to choose a high-quality commercial dog food diet for him. Because there are so many different options available, choosing a dog food can be tricky. Your best bet is to make a direct comparison between two different brands using the ingredients list on the package. For dog food labels, ingredients are listed in descending order by volume – this means that the ingredients at the beginning of the list are present in the highest amount. When evaluating a dog food, you want to see high-quality ingredients at the beginning of the list.

As you already know, protein is the most important nutrient for dogs so you want to see high-quality animal proteins like deboned chicken or turkey meal at the top of an ingredients list. Avoid any product that doesn't start with animal protein from a named source. Meat meals like turkey meal or salmon meal are fine because they are simply pre-cooked proteins and therefore a highly concentrated source of protein. Byproducts and unnamed meat meals (like chicken byproduct meal or poultry meal) are best avoided.

After protein, you want to check the list for digestible carbohydrates and animal-based fats. Whole grains like brown rice and oatmeal are a great option but avoid products made with milled rice or rice bran. You can also choose a gluten- or grain-free product as long as it contains some kind of complex carbohydrate like sweet potato, tapioca, or other fresh fruits and vegetables. Avoid any product made with inexpensive fillers like soy, corn, and wheat ingredients because these ingredients are only used to bulk up the product – they don't actually provide your dog with any significant nutritional value.

When it comes to fats, you want to look for animal sources like chicken fat and salmon oil. Plant-based sources like flaxseed and canola oil are not harmful, but they are less biologically valuable for your dog. You also want to make sure the product offers a blend of both omega-3 and omega-6 fatty acids. Avoid products made with artificial ingredients including flavors, dyes, and preservatives. As a good rule of thumb, avoid any ingredients that you cannot pronounce, especially if it sounds like a chemical.

3.) How Much to Feed Your Great Dane

The amount you need to feed your Great Dane will vary depending on several important factors. Your dog's size is the biggest factor but other things like age and activity level play a role as well. Your Great Dane will need more calories per pound of bodyweight when he is a puppy because he'll need plenty of protein and fat to fuel his growth and development. Once your Great Dane reaches his full size, you then need to feed him just enough to maintain a healthy bodyweight. This can be a difficult path to tread because your dog's calorie needs will vary depending on his age and activity level.

The best way to calculate your Great Dane's energy needs is to calculate his Resting Energy Requirement (RER) first. You can then multiply this number by a certain factor determined by his activity level in order to determine the total number of calories he needs on a daily basis. The formula to calculate your Great Dane's RER is:

RER = 30 x (weight in kg) + 70

For example, if your Great Dane weighed 120 pounds, you would first convert that number into kilograms by dividing it by 2.2 – this would give you a weight of about 54.4 kg. Then, you multiply that number by 30 and add 70. A Great Dane weighing about 120 pounds would have a resting energy requirement of about 1,700 calories per day. Your next step is to use that RER to determine your dog's total calorie needs. To do so, you can use the chart below:

Type of Dog	Daily Calorie Needs
Weight Loss	1.0 x RER
Normal Adult (neutered)	1.6 x RER
Normal Adult (intact)	1.8 x RER
Lightly Active Adult	2.0 x RER
Moderately Active Adult	3.0 x RER
Pregnant (first 42 days)	1.8 x RER
Pregnant (last 21 days)	3.0 x RER
Lactating Female	4.8 x RER
Puppy (2 to 4 months)	3.0 x RER
Puppy (4 to 12 months)	2.0 x RER

As you can see, your Great Dane will need a lot more calories per pound of bodyweight while he is a puppy than he will as an adult dog. Once your Great Dane reaches his maximum size, it is important that you feed him enough calories and protein to maintain a healthy bodyweight but you do not want to overfeed him or he could become obese. You also want to avoid feeding your Great Dane puppy so much that he grows too quickly. If a large-breed puppy grows too fast, it could put extra strain on his bones and joints which will predispose him to musculoskeletal issues as an adult.

Your best bet to keep your Great Dane puppy from growing too fast is to feed him a commercial diet formulated for large-breed puppies. These formulas are made with moderate amounts of protein and fat to prevent overgrowth. Keep your Great Dane puppy on this formula until he reaches about 80% of his maximum size and then switch him over to a large-breed adult formula. Follow the feeding recommendations on the package to determine how much to feed your dog but keep an eye on his weight for a few weeks. If he starts to gain too much weight you might need to cut back. If he loses weight or appears to be lacking in energy, you might need to increase his portion a little bit. You can always ask your vet for advice.

4.) Toxic Foods for Great Danes

When your dog starts begging at the dinner table, it might be tempting to give in and let him have a treat. What many dog owners do not realize, however, is that there are many "people foods" that can be toxic for dogs. <u>Below you will find a list of foods that you should never feed your Great Dane</u>:

- Alcohol
- Apple seeds
- Avocado
- Cherry pits
- Chocolate
- Coffee
- Garlic
- Grapes/raisins
- Hops
- Macadamia nuts
- Mold
- Mushrooms
- Mustard seeds
- Onions/leeks
- Peach pits
- Potato leaves/stems
- Rhubarb leaves
- Tea
- Tomato leaves/stems
- Walnuts
- Xylitol
- Yeast dough

5.) *Toxic Plants for Great Danes*

In addition to being careful about what foods you feed your Great Dane, you also need to be mindful of the plants you keep around the house. There are many common houseplants that are actually toxic to dogs – you may not even realize it. To protect your dog from toxic plants, check the following list then put toxic houseplants out of reach and remove dangerous plants from your property or consider fencing them off.

- Azalea
- Baneberry
- Bird-of-paradise
- Black locust
- Buckeye
- Buttercup
- Caladium
- Castor bean
- Chock-cherries
- Christmas rose
- Common privet
- Cowslip
- Daffodil
- Day lily
- Delphinium
- Easter lily

- Elderberry
- Elephant's ear
- English Ivy
- Foxglove
- Holly
- Horse-chestnut
- Hyacinth
- Iris
- Jack-in-the-pulpit
- Jimsonweed
- Laurels
- Lily of the valley
- Lupines
- May-apple
- Mistletoe
- Morning glory

- Mustards
- Narcissus
- Nightshade
- Oaks
- Oleander
- Philodendron
- Poinsettia
- Poison hemlock
- Potato
- Rhododendron
- Rhubarb
- Sago palm
- Sorghum
- Wild black cherry
- Wild radish
- Wisteria
- Yew

Chapter Seven: Training Your Great Dane

Because the Great Dane is such a giant breed, it takes longer than many other dogs to become fully developed – both physically and mentally. This means that you might have to deal with puppy behavior longer than you would with a smaller breed. One of your most important tasks as a dog owner is to properly train and socialize your dog. In this chapter you will learn the basics about several popular training methods as well as the proper procedure for housetraining your dog. You will also receive tips for teaching basic obedience and tips for dealing with various problem behaviors.

1.) Popular Training Methods

When it comes to dog training, there are a number of different methods to choose from but not all of them are recommended. The Great Dane is an intelligent breed and naturally wants to please his owner, so you do not need to use harsh training methods. In fact, you could severely damage your relationship with your dog if you use punishment-based training methods. Most dog owners recommend using positive-reinforcement to train dogs.

Positive-reinforcement based training methods involve rewarding your dog for good behavior. If you reward your dog for doing something, you can increase the chances that he will do it again. For example, if you want your dog to do his business only in one certain area of the backyard, you can teach him to do so by rewarding him for doing it. This is an important aspect of housetraining which will be covered in the next section.

The key to success with positive-reinforcement training methods is to help your dog identify the desired behavior as quickly as possible. You can give your dog any command you can think of but, unless he knows what that command means, all of your training will be for naught. A simple way to help your dog learn faster is clicker training. To use this type of training your hold the clicker in one hand and use your other hand to guide your dog to perform the desired behavior. When he does the behavior, you immediately click the clicker then issue the reward. It should only take a few repetitions for your dog to learn what behavior you are targeting.

2.) Housetraining Your Great Dane

Many dog experts agree that crate training is the most effective method of housetraining for dogs. This method is quite simple and, if you do it right, your dog will learn to like being in his crate instead of viewing it as a form of punishment. The secret lies in getting your puppy used to the crate before you start training. You can do this by feeding him his meals in the crate and by tossing treats and toys into it as a kind of game until he becomes completely comfortable with the crate. You also want to encourage him to take naps in the crate so he learns that it is a special place he can call his own.

Once your puppy is used to the crate you can start using it for housetraining. When you are at home, keep your puppy in the same room with you at all times and monitor him closely. Take him outside once every hour or so, especially right after meals and after he wakes up from a nap. You should also take him outside if you see him showing signs that he has to go – he might start sniffing the ground, turning in circles, or squatting.

When you take your puppy outside, take him to a designated portion of the yard each time – you want to teach him to only do his business in this area. When you take your puppy out, give him a verbal command like "Go pee" that he will learn to associate with the action. If your puppy does his business, praise him excitedly and offer him a treat. If he does not, simply bring him back inside and try again in a little bit. The more consistent you are in following this sequence, the faster your puppy will learn what is expected of him when you take him out.

The other aspect to this type of training involves confining your puppy to the crate overnight and when you are not at home. If the crate is properly sized, your puppy will view it as his "den" and dogs have a natural aversion to soiling their dens. You want to be careful not to keep your puppy confined to the crate for longer than he is physically capable of holding his bladder. At first this may only be an hour or two but that time will increase as your puppy gets older. Just make sure your let him outside immediately after releasing him from the crate and before you confine him.

The key to housetraining, as with any kind of training, is consistency. You need to reward and praise your puppy every time he does his business in the designated area if you want him to learn. Do not punish your puppy for having an accident, however, because he is unlikely to connect the punishment to the behavior and he might just learn to fear you. When properly executed, many dogs become housetrained in a matter of weeks.

3.) Teaching Basic Commands

Not only can positive reinforcement be used for housetraining, but you can also apply it to teaching your Great Dane basic commands. Again, the key is to make sure that your dog knows which behavior it is that you are requesting so he can perform it. Below you will find tips for teaching the four basic commands: Sit, Down, Come, and Stay.

Sit

Start by kneeling in front of your puppy and hold a treat in your dominant hand, pinching it between the thumb and forefinger. Hold the treat in front of your puppy's nose and tell him "Sit" in a firm tone. Immediately move the treat forward and up, toward the back of your puppy's head. He should lift his nose the follow the treat and, in doing so, lower his bottom to the floor. When his bottom hits the ground, immediately tell him "Good!" and give him the treat. Repeat this process several times until your puppy gets the hang of it. Once he does, you can start cutting back, offering the treat only every other time. Just be sure to praise your puppy every time he performs the desired behavior.

Down

Start by kneeling in front of your puppy and hold a treat in your dominant hand, pinching it between the thumb and forefinger. Hold the treat in front of your puppy's nose and tell him "Sit" in a firm tone. When he does, tell him "Good" but do not give him the treat yet. Instead, lower the treat quickly to the ground between your puppy's feet, tell him "Down" – he should follow it with his nose and, in doing so, lower his body to the ground. If he does, tell him "Good and give him the treat. If he doesn't, return to the beginning and try again.

Come

Start by kneeling in front of your puppy and hold a treat in your dominant hand, pinching it between the thumb and forefinger. Hold the treat in front of your puppy's nose and tell him "Come!" in an excited tone while taking a quick step backwards, away from him. If your puppy follows you, tell him "Good" and give him the treat. Repeat the sequence several times then gradually start to increase the distance you move away from your puppy before you reward him. This type of training relies on your puppy's desire to come to you, so you should make sure to play with your puppy so you foster a healthy relationship.

having your puppy sit down and ask a
...u or family member to hold onto his collar. Stand in
front of your puppy and hold the treat in front of his nose
then give him the "Sit" command and praise him when he
responds correctly. Next, say "Stay" in a firm tone and take
a few steps backward away from your puppy while
holding up your opposite hand. Pause for a moment then
come back to your puppy and praise and reward him.
Repeat this sequence several times, praising and rewarding
your puppy when he stays put. After a few repetitions you
can increase the distance you move away from your puppy
each time you give the command.

4.) Dealing with Problem Behaviors

While many dog owners believe that the key to stopping bad behaviors is to punish their dog for doing them, it is infinitely more effective to redirect those behaviors to a more appropriate outlet. Think about this – chewing is a natural behavior for dogs so if you try to eliminate this behavior entirely by punishing your dog for chewing on things, you are changing your dog's nature. You might be able to stop your dog from chewing on that one thing, but you will have trouble getting him to stop chewing on things entirely. It would be better for you to teach your dog what he is and is not allowed to chew on.

To deal with problem behaviors, you have to redirect your dog. For example, if you find your dog chewing on one of your shoes you would take the shoe away and tell your dog "No" in a firm voice so he learns that you do not approve of him chewing on your shoe. Instead of leaving it at that, however, you would then give your dog a chew toy and encourage him to chew on that instead. When he does, you would praise and reward him for doing it. In doing so, you are teaching your dog that he gets a reward for chewing on his toys but he doesn't get one for chewing on your shoes. Which one do you think your dog is more likely to do in the future? This type of training can be applied to all kinds of behavioral problems – you just have to redirect the problem behavior.

Chapter Eight: Grooming Your Great Dane

The Great Dane may have a very short coat but, like all dogs, he still sheds. Brushing your dog's coat on a regular basis is a very important task, but it is not the only grooming task you will need to fulfill. In this chapter you will learn the basics about grooming your Great Dane including tips for bathing and brushing as well as step-by-step guides for trimming your dog's nails and cleaning his ears. It is important that you take care of your Great Dane by performing these simple tasks because neglecting them can lead to big problems in the future.

1.) Recommended Tools and Methods

Because the Great Dane has such a short coat, maintenance is fairly easy. Like all dogs, however, Great Danes do shed so you should still brush your dog several times a week to keep shedding to a minimum. The best grooming tool to use for Great Danes is a rubber curry comb. You simply hold the comb in one hand and run it along your dog's body in the direction of hair growth. You'll have to stop once in a while to remove accumulated hair from the comb.

In addition to brushing your Great Dane's coat several times a week you may need to bathe him once in a while as well. To bathe your dog, fill your bathtub with several inches of lukewarm water then have your dog get into the tub. Wet him down thoroughly with a spray hose or by pouring water over him – you may need to use your hands to work the water into his coat. Just be sure to keep his head dry – you don't want to get any water into his ears, nose or eyes.

Once your dog's coat is thoroughly wetted, squeeze a little bit of dog-friendly shampoo onto his back and work it into a lather. When you are ready to rinse, be sure to get all of the soap residue out of your dog's coat so it doesn't dry out his skin. Then towel your dog's coat to remove most of the moisture then let him air-dry. If it is cold out, you might need to use a blow dryer on the lowest heat setting to completely dry your dog's coat. You can then clean your dog's face separately with a damp cloth.

2.) Trimming Your Dog's Nails

Trimming your Great Dane's nails is very important because overgrown nails can cause a number of problems. You need to be very careful when trimming your dog's nails, however, because the nail contains a blood vessel called the quick – if you cut the nail too short you could sever the quick. This will not only cause profuse bleeding, but it will be painful for your dog as well. Your best bet is to only trim the pointed tip of the nail and to do so once every week or two. Before you trim your dog's nails for the first time you should have a professional groomer or your vet show you the proper technique.

3.) Cleaning Your Dog's Ears

In addition to trimming your dog's nails once every week or two, you should also keep his ears clean. The frequency with which you clean your Great Dane's ears may vary depending on whether his ears are cropped or not. If your Great Dane's ears are cropped, they will stand erect and get plenty of airflow which will reduce his risk for ear infections. If you leave your dog's ears natural, however, they will hang down over the sides of his head and they will retain moisture, increasing the risk for infections. For Great Danes with floppy ears, you should clean the ears weekly.

In order to clean your dog's ears properly you should purchase dog ear cleaner and soft cotton balls or pads. Squeeze a few drops of the solution into your dog's ear canal and gently massage the base of the ear to distribute the solution. Then, just use the cotton ball or pad to wipe away any debris from the ear as well as the excess solution. To reduce your dog's risk for ear infections, make sure to keep his ears clean and dry.

Chapter Nine: Breeding Great Danes

Making the decision to breed your Great Dane is not a choice that should be taken lightly. Not only will you have to provide for a pregnant dog and a litter of puppies, but you will also be putting your dog at risk for complications. Before you decide whether or not to breed your Great Dane, take the time to learn everything you can about the breeding process to make sure you fully understand the risks you will be taking with your dog. If you decide that you definitely want to breed your Great Dane, the information in this chapter will help get you started on the right path.

1.) Basic Breeding Information

Choosing to breed your Great Dane is not something you should do on a whim. Not only does it take a great deal of time and money, but breeding a dog does come with risks. If your only reason for breeding your Great Dane is to earn some extra money by selling the puppies, think again. Most hobby breeders admit that, by the time they pay for veterinary costs and raise the pups enough to sell them, they are lucky to come out even on costs. You should only breed your Great Dane if your goal is to improve the breed. Even then you need to be very careful about which dogs you select to breed and you need to run plenty of health checks to make sure you won't be passing on any congenital conditions to the puppies.

If you meet the criteria for being a responsible breeder, your next move is to learn everything you can about breeding Great Danes. Breeding one dog breed is similar to breeding any other, but there are some specific details about breeding Great Danes that you need to know. For example, because Great Danes are such a large breed, they take a lot of time to mature – you should never breed a male Great Dane before the age of 1 year and the minimum breeding age for females is 2 years. If you breed your Great Danes too early not only could you be putting them at a greater risk for complications, but the AKC is unlikely to accept the litter for registration – this means you'll have a harder time selling the puppies.

Great Danes are known or producing very large litters – as many as sixteen puppies at one time. Although this breed can have sixteen or more puppies in a litter, the average number of puppies is 6 to 8. Having a litter of puppies that large can be very taxing on the mother so be absolutely sure you want to put your bitch at risk before you start breeding. You also have to consider that caring for such a large litter of puppies will be no easy task. If you decide that breeding your Great Dane is not the right choice, be sure to have your dog spayed or neutered before six months of age.

2.) The Breeding Process

One of the most important concepts you need to understand regarding the breeding process for Great Danes is the estrus cycle. The estrus cycle, also known as heat, is the cycle during which a female dog becomes fertile and receptive to breeding. Most female dogs go into heat twice a year, though it may not be exactly six months in between – it takes a few years for a dog's cycle to normalize. Large dogs like the Great Dane may not experience their first heat until 18 to 24 months of age. This is very late compared to small-breed dogs which typically reach sexual maturity around 6 months of age.

The estrus cycle in dogs typically lasts for 2 to 3 weeks. The cycle begins when the vulva starts to swell – this may be followed by a pinkish discharge. When the discharge becomes completely clear (or stops completely) and the vulva returns to normal, it is the end of the estrus cycle. When a female is in heat she is likely to urinate more frequently – she may also spray urine on household objects as a means of marking her territory. You need to be very careful about taking your dog outside when she is in heat because male dogs can smell her from great distances and will do anything they can to mate with her. You want to make sure that only the male you have chosen mates with your female.

Throughout the estrus cycle, the vaginal discharge will become more watery. When the discharge is light pink and watery (this occurs around the 10th day of the cycle), the female will be the most fertile. She will start to ovulate and may also become receptive to the advances of the male dog. If you have planned a breeding, this is when you should introduce the female to the male dog. If the female is receptive, the male will mount her from behind and ejaculate into her. The male's sperm can survive in the female's reproductive tract for up to 5 days so, technically, she could become pregnant even if she is bred earlier in the cycle. To ensure conception you may choose to unite the male and female multiple times during one cycle.

If the mating is successful, conception will occur and the female dog will become pregnant. Again, Great Dane litters can have as many as 16 puppies, though 6 to 8 is the average number. Still, it is not uncommon for a Great Dane to give birth to a dozen puppies at a time. Once the female becomes pregnant, she will endure a gestation period lasting about 63 days, or nine weeks. It won't be until the third week of pregnancy, however, that you will actually be able to tell the dog is pregnant.

3.) Raising Great Dane Puppies

After about three weeks of gestation it will start to become obvious that the bitch is pregnant. By day 28 it will be safe to have a veterinarian palpate the female's abdomen to detect the puppies. It is safe to perform an ultrasound as early as 25 days, though you should wait until about six weeks to use x-ray. Be sure to take your pregnant female to the vet for regular checkups throughout her pregnancy and follow your vet's advice for care.

You should not have to increase the amount you are feeding your Great Dane until the fourth or fifth week of gestation. Just to be safe, however, it would be a good idea to offer your dog free feeding – she will know how much she needs to eat and this will help to prevent under-feeding. When you do increase your female dog's rations you do not need to increase them significantly – the increase should be proportional to the amount of weight your dog has gained. Again, you can ask your vet for recommendations.

Around the eighth week of pregnancy you should start preparing for the birth. Provide your dog with a whelping box – a comfortable area that is dark and quiet. You can line the area with old towels and blankets to keep your dog comfortable. Over the next few days leading up to the start of labor, your dog will start to spend more and more time in the whelping box. This is when you should start checking your dog's internal temperature. The normal temperature range is between 100°F and 102°F (37.7°C to 38.8°C). When the temperature starts to drop, it is an indication that labor will begin within 24 hours.

When your Great Dane goes into labor, she will show obvious signs of discomfort such as pacing restlessly and panting. The early stages of labor for dogs can last for several hours and contractions may occur as often as every 10 minutes. Contraction typically occur in waves of three to five followed by a period of rest. If your Great Dane has more than two hours of contractions without whelping any puppies, it may be a sign of dangerous complications and you should take her to the vet immediately.

Once your female begins to whelp, she will deliver one puppy approximately every thirty minutes after between ten and thirty minutes of straining. After each puppy is born, the mother will lick the puppy clean and sever the umbilical cord with her teeth. When she licks the puppy it will not only clean him – it also stimulates him to start breathing on his own. Your dog should do this automatically without your help, but you should still be nearby in case there is a problem. Once all of the puppies have been born the female will expel the remainder of the placenta and then the puppies will begin nursing.

It is essential that your puppies begin nursing as soon as possible after delivery because the first milk the mother produces is full of antibodies. These antibodies will protect the puppies until their own immune systems have time to develop. The first milk the mother produces is called the colostrum. Over the next few weeks, the puppies will spend most of their time nursing and sleeping. Around 3 weeks of age, the puppies will open their eyes and they will start to become more active, playing with each other and exploring the area outside the whelping box. As long as the female produces enough milk, the puppies will grow fairly quickly.

By six weeks of age you should start helping the mother wean the puppies if she has not done so already. Begin by offering the puppies small amounts of large-breed puppy food soaked in water or broth. The puppies may begin to sample the food without your help but if they haven't been weaned by six weeks of age you will need to step in. The puppies should be fully weaned by 8 weeks and this is when you can start to pair them up with their new owners. Before sending your puppies off to their new home, make sure they are fully weaned, updated on vaccines, and socialized.

Chapter Ten: Keeping Your Dog Healthy

Nothing is more heartbreaking than seeing your furry friend and companion not feeling well. The Great Dane is a very healthy breed in general, but all dogs are prone to developing certain health problems or hereditary conditions over time. The best thing you can do for your dog is educate yourself about matters of health so you can be prepared to deal with illnesses when they occur. In this chapter you will learn about the conditions to which the Great Dane is prone. You will also receive information about preventing illness through vaccinations, about nutritional deficiencies, and about pet insurance.

1.) Common Great Dane Health Problems

The most important thing you can do to keep your Great Dane healthy is to provide him with a high-quality, nutritious diet. Even if you do feed your dog a top-of-the-line dog food, however, he may still be susceptible to certain diseases or hereditary conditions. The key to making sure your Great Dane recovers quickly and fully when he gets sick is to familiarize yourself with all of the different conditions that have the potential to affect this breed. The more you know, the better you will be able to identify symptoms to make a diagnosis and the faster you will be able to get your dog the treatment he needs.

Below you will find a list of some of the most common conditions affecting the Great Dane breed. You will also receive an in-depth overview of each condition including causes, symptoms, and treatment options:

- Aortic Stenosis
- Bone Cancer
- Dilated Cardiomyopathy
- Entropion
- Gastric Dilation Volvulus
- Heartworm
- Hip Dysplasia
- Hypertrophic Osteodystrophy
- Wobbler's Disease

Aortic Stenosis

This condition is characterized by the narrowing of the aortic valve. When the valve narrows it causes a blockage of blood flow to the heart and that leads to a host of other problems. Aortic stenosis can be mild, moderate, or severe and it is most commonly seen in large-breed dogs like the Great Dane. This condition typically doesn't produce any symptoms in mild cases but, in more severe cases, you may notice symptoms like weakness, difficulty breathing, fainting, or even sudden death.

In mild cases of aortic stenosis, the dog has a good chance of recovering, though it is not recommended that the dog be bred. In more severe cases, treatments will be geared toward controlling and improving heart function. Medications may be given to keep the heart from beating too fast and to prevent arrhythmias. In some cases, surgery may be performed to reduce the obstruction. No matter what kind of treatment your dog receives, follow-up examinations are essential to monitor his progress as he recovers from the disease.

Bone Cancer

Also known as osteosarcoma, bone cancer is unfortunately fairly common in Great Danes and the risk for this condition increases with age. The bones most commonly affected by osteosarcoma are the weight-bearing bones in the legs and rapid growth will increase the dog's risk for developing the disease. Many veterinarian researchers believe that strenuous activity, particularly during youth, causes microscopic fractures in the bones which then leads to cancer formation.

There are several options for treatment of osteosarcoma and the right treatment will depend on the presentation of the disease. In some cases, chemotherapy is prescribed, though this is usually a secondary treatment that follows amputation of the affected limb. Some of the most common symptoms of bone cancer in dogs include progressive lameness, pain, lethargy or weakness, swelling of the leg, and broken bones. Many dogs also lose their appetite or have difficulty eating.

Though there are treatment options available for osteosarcoma in dogs, the prognosis is generally not very good. In most cases, dogs will eventually succumb to the disease, regardless of treatment. Once the dog develops bone cancer, it generally has 4 to 5 months to live after the limb has been amputated.

Dilated Cardiomyopathy

Sometimes shortened to DCM, dilated cardiomyopathy is a condition characterized by an enlarged heart. In most cases, both the upper and lower chambers of the heart become enlarged, though one side may be more affected than the other. When the heart becomes enlarged, its ability to pump blood to the lungs and to the other internal organs becomes affected and the body starts to deteriorate. Fluid starts to accumulate in the lungs which leads to difficulty breathing and abdominal distension. Eventually, the dog may lose consciousness.

The cause of dilated cardiomyopathy in dogs is largely unknown, but certain nutritional deficiencies are thought to play a role. Deficiencies of taurine or carnitine, for example, have been implicated in cases of DCM in certain breeds, while others simply have a genetic predisposition. Treatment options for DCM are typically focused on improving heart function and toward treating the signs of heart failure. Medical treatments may be used to help increase heart contractions and to slow rapid breathing – diuretics may also be prescribed to reduce fluid accumulation in the lungs. In most cases, long-term hospitalization is not necessary.

Entropion

One of the most common eye problems seen in dogs is entropion. This condition is genetic and it occurs when part of the eyelid becomes inverted, or folded in. Ectropion, a similar condition, occurs when the lower eyelid turns outward. Though entropion is primarily an inherited condition, it can also be secondary to eye infections or trauma to the eye. When the eyelid rolls inward, it generally causes hair on the eyelid to rub against the cornea – this results in pain and irritation in most cases but it can also lead to corneal erosion or lesions.

Entropion is highly treatable, though surgery is generally the only option. Surgical correction of this condition involves removing a section of skin from the eyelid in order to roll it back into place. Once this heals, the dog may require a second or third surgery to reduce the risk of over-correction and to keep the problem from recurring later. In most cases, veterinarians will not perform the surgery until the dog reaches its maximum size – this can occur as late as 18 months for Great Danes which, unfortunately, means the dog might have to deal with the pain and irritation for a while if he develops entropion at a very early age.

Gastric Dilation Volvulus

Also known as bloat or gastric torsio
dilation volvulus is a very serious disease t
affects large-breed dogs like the Great Dane. This condition
occurs when the dog's stomach dilates (or swells) and the
abdomen fills with air. When this happens, the stomach
may actually twist on its axis which may cut off blood flow
to the stomach and other internal organs. This torsion can
also lead to increased pressure in the abdomen, distension
of the stomach, and even cardiovascular damage. If blood
flow to the organs is not restored, it could lead to organ
failure and even death.

The symptoms of bloat (aside from the bloating, of
course) include abdominal pain, depression, anxiety,
collapse, excessive drooling, dry heaving, or vomiting. As
the condition gets worse, your dog might have a weak
pulse and labored breathing. The exact cause of this
condition is unknown, but it is most likely to occur when
deep-chested dogs eat too much or too quickly – it can also
occur if the dog drinks a lot of water too soon after a meal
or if he is subjected to vigorous exercise after eating.
Feeding your dog smaller meals throughout the day can
help to prevent this condition and feeding him from a
raised bowl may also help.

Heartworm

Heartworm is a very serious disease but, fortunately, it is also very easy to prevent. This disease is not actually caused by a worm but by a parasitic roundworm nicknamed heartworm because that is the organ that it infects. Heartworms can only be transmitted to dogs through the bite of an infected mosquito – the mosquito passes the heartworm eggs into the dog's bloodstream through the bite and the eggs mature in the dog's bloodstream until they develop into adult heartworms in the dog's heart.

Once your dog has been bitten by an infected mosquito, it takes about six months for the baby heartworms to mature. Once they do, the heartworms can actually live inside your dog for as long as 5 to 7 years. During the early stages of the disease, your dog is unlikely to show any symptoms. As the disease progresses, however, your dog may show signs of exercise reluctance, persistent cough, decreased appetite, and weight loss. Later, the disease may also progress to fluid in the belly and heart failure. Without surgical intervention, the dog is unlikely to survive. Fortunately, heartworm is easily prevented by giving your dog a monthly pill that you can get with a prescription from your vet.

Hip Dysplasia

Large-breed dogs like the Great Dane have an increased risk for developing musculoskeletal problems like hip dysplasia. If your puppy grows too quickly while he is young it could lead to developmental issues that could put him at an increased risk for hip dysplasia – there are also some genetic factors in play. Hip dysplasia occurs when the hip joint is malformed, causing the femoral head to pop in and out of socket. Not only does this result in pain for your dog, but it can also lead to osteoarthritis in the affected joint.

Hip dysplasia occurs in dogs of all different ages and it can develop as early as several months of age. The most common symptoms of hip dysplasia include altered gait (particularly while running), a hopping gait, trouble navigating stairs, reluctance to exercise, stiffness or soreness in the limb, and eventually lameness. In many cases the dog will act completely normal when the femoral head is in place – he may only display these symptoms when the bone pops out of joint.

If your Great Dane is genetically predisposed to hip dysplasia you may not be able to prevent it from happening. The only permanent solution is surgical repair of the joint or total hip replacement. Medical treatments may be helpful to reduce pain and inflammation.

Hypertrophic Osteodystrophy

Sometimes simply called bone inflammation, hypertrophic osteodystrophy is a condition that affects the front limbs of large-breed puppies. This condition usually strikes between the ages of 3 and 6 months and it is most likely to occur if your Great Dane puppy grows too quickly. Some of the most common symptoms of the disease include painful swelling of the growth plates in the bone, particularly in the radius, ulna, and tibia. Your dog may also show signs of lethargy, reluctance to move, loss of appetite, and fever.

Hypertrophic osteodystrophy is generally diagnosed through a combination of physical exam and x-rays. The main treatments for this condition are supportive, involving medical treatment with anti-inflammatories and pain medication. Unfortunately, there is no known cause for this condition which means that it is difficult to prevent. It is thought, however, that maintaining a healthy diet high in vitamin C may help to prevent the condition. Preventing your large-breed puppy from growing too quickly can also reduce his risk for hypertrophic dystrophy.

Wobbler's Disease

Also known as Wobbler's Syndrome, Wobbler's disease is commonly seen in large- and giant-breed dogs. This condition is technically called cervical spondylomyelopathy (CSM) because it affects the cervical spine of the dog. This condition occurs when the spinal cord becomes compressed – this leads to neck pain and, in many cases, to neurological symptoms. The name Wobbler's Disease was given in reference to the wobbling gait shown by many affected dogs.

In addition to a wobbling gait, many dogs affected by this condition show signs of neck pain or stiffness, weakness, shortened gait, partial or complete paralysis, and difficulty rising. There are a number of factors thought to contribute to this disease include rapid growth in large-breed puppies and nutritional factors such as excess protein and calcium.

Treatment options for this condition vary depending on the severity of the condition. Surgical treatments can help to relieve spinal compression, though medical treatments may be preferred in minor cases. In most cases, the dog needs several weeks of rest which may necessitate bladder catheterization so the dog doesn't have to go outside to relieve himself. Physical therapy may also be a part of the treatment.

2.) Preventing Illness – Vaccinations

As you have already learned, the most important thing you can do to keep your Great Dane healthy is to feed him a high-quality diet. Another important thing you can do to prevent illness is to have your dog vaccinated. Depending where you live, your dog's risk for certain diseases may be higher than in other areas so be sure to check with your veterinarian to see which vaccines your dog actually needs.

On the following page you will find a chart detailing the most common vaccines for dogs as well as the recommended times they should have them:

Recommended Vaccination Schedule			
Vaccine	Doses	Age	Booster
Rabies	1	12 weeks	annually
Distemper	3	6 to 16 weeks	3 years
Parvovirus	3	6 to 16 weeks	3 years
Adenovirus	3	6 to 16 weeks	3 years
Parainfluenza	3	6 weeks, 12 to 14 weeks	3 years
Bordetella	1	6 weeks	annually
Lyme Disease	2	9, 13 to 14 weeks	annually
Leptospirosis	2	12 and 16 weeks	annually
Canine Influenza	2	6 to 8, 8 to 12 weeks	annually

3.) The Importance of Diet – Nutritional Deficiencies

You have already learned about the importance of a healthy diet for Great Danes but you may not yet understand the importance of certain nutrients. If your dog's diet isn't properly formulated he may not get enough of certain vitamins or minerals which could put him at risk for nutritional deficiencies. In this section you will learn about the top five most common nutritional deficiencies affecting dogs including symptoms and the recommended treatment options.

Vitamin A Deficiency – Vitamin A is a fat-soluble vitamin that can be found in dairy products as well as liver and certain yellow vegetables. Vitamin A is needed for the development of strong bones and teeth – it also affects the health of your dog's skin and coat. Vitamin A deficiencies may cause stunted growth and poor development – they might also lead to skin problems, poor coat, eye problems, and immune system problems.

Vitamin E Deficiency – Vitamin E is another fat-soluble vitamin and it comes from vegetable oil, leafy greens, wheat germ, and liver. Vitamin E helps the dog's body metabolize fats and it supports general cell function. Vitamin E deficiencies can cause liver problems and reproductive disorders as well as problems with the muscle, nerves, heart, and eyes.

Calcium Deficiency – Calcium is an important mineral for your dog's heart and muscle as well as nerve function. Deficiencies in calcium (or a calcium-phosphorus imbalance) can lead to lameness or spasms as well as heart palpitations, bone fractures, high blood pressure, and arthritis. Calcium deficiencies are usually caused by a high-meat diet because fresh meat is high in potassium.

Iron Deficiency – Also known as iron deficiency anemia, iron deficiency occurs when the dog doesn't have enough red blood cells to carry the necessary oxygen supply to his muscles and organs. Symptoms of iron deficiency include stunted growth, loss of appetite, lethargy, depression, rapid breathing, and dark stools.

Magnesium Deficiency – Magnesium is required for the maintenance of healthy metabolic function, so a magnesium deficiency is very serious for your dog. Symptoms of magnesium deficiency include depression, weakness, trembling, loss of coordination, and changes in behavior. Though magnesium deficiency is very dangerous, so is magnesium overdose so you need to be very careful when treating this type of deficiency.

4.) Pet Insurance – Do You Need It?

Owning and caring for a dog can be very expensive, especially when it comes to vet bills. Because vet costs can be so high, many Great Dane owners consider buying a pet insurance policy. Before you start shopping around for policies, take a moment to learn what pet insurance is and to think about the pros and cons. In this section you will learn the basics about pet insurance so you can make an informed decision for yourself.

Pet insurance plans are like health insurance plans but for pets. In essence, they exist to help mitigate your out-of-pocket costs for veterinary care. Just like health insurance, different companies offer different plans and each plan has its own set of benefits and restrictions. Some pet insurance plans only cover accidents while others cover preventive care and illnesses. Make sure you read the details of each plan before you purchase one so you can be sure the services you want are covered.

The main difference between pet insurance plans and health insurance plans (aside from the fact that they are for pets, not people) is in the way the plan pays benefits. Health insurance plans issue payments directly to the provider on your behalf. Pet insurance plans, on the other hand, offer reimbursement for covered services. This means that you have to pay the bills upfront but you will then receive reimbursement for covered services. Most plans offer reimbursement for up to 90% of covered costs.

Pet insurance might sound like a great idea but it is not always worth it. If your pet is very healthy, for example, you could end up paying a monthly premium without ever using your benefits. If you purchase a puppy plan, however, you might save a lot of money on the cost of spay/neuter surgery and initial vaccinations. Other plans only offer catastrophic coverage – they might have low premiums but higher deductibles. Before you shop around for plans, take a moment to consider your needs and then compare costs.

Below you will find a chart to use as an example when shopping around for pet insurance plans:

Estimated Cost for Pet Insurance Plans**			
Pet Wellness Plan	Injury Plan (Emergency)	Medical Plan (Economical)	Major Medical Plan
$18 - $34/mo (£16 – £30)	$10/mo (£9/mo)	$19-$27/mo (£17 to £24)	$25-$35/mo (£23 to £32)

Wellness exams, Vaccinations, Dental Cleaning	Injuries only (like poison and broken bones)	Basic coverage for accidents, emergencies, and illness	Double benefits of Medical Plan
3 levels (max, plus, basic)	Max yearly benefit limit $14,000 (£12,600)	Max yearly benefit limit $7,000 (£6,300)	Max yearly benefit limit $14,000 (£12,600)

**This information is taken from Veterinary Pet Insurance, a division of Nationwide Insurance. Prices are subject to change and are only intended to give a general idea of pricing and coverage options for pet insurance plans.

Chapter Eleven: Showing Your Great Dane

If you are looking for a way to increase the bond between you and your Great Dane, you might want to consider showing your dog. Participating in dog shows is a wonderful experience for dogs and their owners – it can also be an exciting challenge. Most dog shows are reserved for purebred dogs and you need to make sure your dog possesses the ideal qualities for the breed before you attempt to show him. You will learn all about the Great Dane breed standard in this chapter and you will receive general tips for showing your dog.

1.) Great Dane Breed Standard

Before you even think about showing your Great Dane, you need to determine whether or not he is a good example of the breed standard. Breed standards for dogs are set forth by the AKC and the Kennel Club in Europe. These breed standards offer the set of characteristics to which purebred specimens of the breed are compared during dog shows. <u>You will find an overview of the AKC breed standard for the Great Dane below</u>:

General Appearance – The Great Dane is regal in appearance, exhibiting great size and strength with a well-formed and smoothly muscled body. The conformation should be balanced so it does not appear clumsy.

Size, Proportion and Substance – The male is more massive than the bitch, having a larger frame and heavier bones. The male shouldn't be less than 30 inches at the shoulder but 32 inches is preferable. The female shouldn't be less than 28 inches at the shoulder, but 30 inches is preferable. The ratio of length to height should be square. Dogs under minimum height will be disqualified.

Head and Neck – The head is long and rectangular, the plane of the muzzle straight and parallel. The eyes are medium-sized, dark, and deep-set with an intelligent expression. The ears are medium in size and high-set, folded close to the cheek. The neck is firm, muscular and well arched.

Body and Legs – The tail is set high, broad at the base and tapering to the hock joint. The forequarters are strong and muscular, as are the hindquarters. The feet are round and compact with well-arched toes.

Coat and Color – Coat should be short and thick with a glossy appearance. There are six accepted colors/patterns:

- **Brindle**: Base color of yellow-gold with strong black cross stripes in a chevron pattern. Black mask is preferable.
- **Fawn**: Base color of yellow-gold with a black mask. White markings on the chest and toes are undesirable.
- **Blue**: An overall color of pure steel blue – no white markings.
- **Black**: An overall color of glossy black – no white markings.

- **Harlequin**: Base color of pure white with irregular, torn black patches over the whole body. Pure white neck is preferable and merle patches are normal.
- **Mantle**: A black-and-white color with a solid black blanket over the whole body. Black skull with white muzzle, optional white blaze.

Gait – Long, easy strides to denote strength and power. No twisting of the elbows or hock joints.

Temperament – Friendly and dependable, courageous and spirited – never aggressive or timid.

Disqualifications – There are only four characteristics which result in disqualification for the Great Dane. These include split note, under minimum height, docked tail, and any color other than those described.

2.) Preparing Your Dog for Show

The first step in preparing your dog for show is to ensure that he meets the breed standard. Depending where you live, the breed standard may vary slightly – there is both an AKC version and a Kennel Club version of the Great Dane Standard. In addition to making sure your dog meets the breed standard you should familiarize yourself with the rules of the show you intend to enter. Rules and restrictions will vary from one show to another, so make sure you have a thorough understanding of them before you enter your dog. <u>To help you get an idea, make sure your dog meets the following general requirements</u>:

- Your Great Dane should be completely housetrained – this shouldn't be a problem as long as your dog meets the age requirements for the show.

- Your dog should be fully socialized and capable of getting along with other dogs and humans.

- Your Great Dane needs to have basic obedience training and he needs to listen and respond to your commands.

- Your dog should be gentle and even-tempered, unlikely to act aggressive or timid in a public setting.

- Your Great Dane should be caught up on necessary vaccinations to ensure that he doesn't catch or pass on a disease to other dogs at the show.

In addition to ensuring that your Great Dane meets both the general and specific show requirements you should also pack a show kit. This kit will include all of the things you and your dog will need on the day of the show. Some things you might want to bring include:

- Your dog's registration and license information
- A dog crate, bed and exercise pen
- Food and water bowls for your dog
- Your dog's food and treats
- Grooming supplies and grooming table (if needed)
- Any medications your dog is taking
- Toys to keep your dog occupied
- A change of clothes for yourself
- Food and water for yourself
- Paper towels or rags and trash bags for cleanup

Chapter Twelve: Frequently Asked Questions

Becoming a dog owner is a big responsibility, so you need to make sure that you are up to the task before you go pick out a puppy. Hopefully, in reading this book, you have learned as much as you ever wanted to know about the Great Dane breed and its care requirements. If you still have questions, however, that is okay! The best dog owners are the ones that constantly seek knowledge about providing their dogs with the top degree of care. In this chapter you will find a collection of frequently asked questions regarding Great Danes and dog ownership to help you become the best dog owner you can be.

Q: *Are Great Danes a good choice for beginners?*

A: The Great Dane is generally not what you would consider a high-maintenance dog but it is not necessarily the easiest breed to own either. These dogs grow very large so they need a lot of space. They also tend to develop slowly, so you may have to deal with puppy behavior for longer than you would with another breed. This is not to say that a beginner could not keep a Great Dane, but it will generally be easier for an experienced dog owner to adapt to these things.

Q: *Do Great Danes shed a lot?*

A: All dogs shed – it is a fact of life. The Great Dane has a short coat, however, and it is not a double coat, so it sheds less than many breeds. Still, you need to brush your dog's coat several times a week in order to keep shedding to a minimum.

Q: *Is it easy to train a Great Dane?*

A: The Great Dane may not be at the top of the intelligence list for dog breeds, but it is still a smart dog. These dogs take to training well as long as positive reinforcement methods are used and as long as the dog is properly motivated to earn his owner's love. Forming a strong bond with your Great Dane is essential for good training.

Q: *What kind of dog food do you recommend?*

A: In the chapter about dog nutrition you learned the basics about your dog's nutritional needs and received tips for shopping for dog food. If you still need more help, however, you can start with some high-quality brands like Blue Buffalo, Canidae, Addiction, or Acana. Remember, look for a product made with high-quality ingredients that is formulated for large-breed dogs.

Q: *Should I get a male or female dog?*

A: The answer to this question is not a simple "Yes" or "No" because it largely depends on preference. Generally speaking, male dogs are a little more emotionally stable but they tend to be more independent and aggressive (especially when not properly trained or socialized). Female dogs, generally speaking, are less pushy and they can be very affectionate. In general, however, temperament and personality depends on the individual.

Q: *Do I have to get a purebred Great Dane?*

A: The alternative to a purebred Great Dane is a crossbreed – that is, a Great Dane crossed with one or more other breeds. Crossbreed dogs can make great pets, just like purebreds, but you will be taking a gamble in terms of their health. It is harder to track the pedigree of crossbreed dogs and, in many cases, they are the result of an accidental breeding. If you want to be certain of your Great Dane's health and breeding, purchasing a purebred puppy from a responsible breeder is the way to go. If you aren't concerned about showing or breeding your Great Dane, however, a crossbreed might be perfectly fine.

Q: *Do Great Danes slobber a lot?*

A: It varies from one dog to another but Great Danes do have a tendency to drool a bit – especially after eating or drinking. When you take your dog out you may want to take a small towel or cloth around to keep him cleaned up.

Q: *What benefits does spaying/neutering provide?*

A: Unless you plan to breed your Great Dane you should definitely have your dog spayed or neutered before the age of six months. Having your dog spayed/neutered will reduce the volatility of his or her temperament to some degree but the main benefits are in regards to health.

Having your female dog spayed before 6 months will prevent uterine infections and reduce the risk for ovarian and breast cancer. Neutering a male dog before 6 months will reduce urine marking behavior as well as aggression or dominance – it will also reduce his risk for prostate and testicular cancers.

Chapter Thirteen: Great Dane Care Sheet

By now you should have a thorough understanding of the Great Dane breed and you probably already know whether or not it is the right breed for you. If you've decided that the Great Dane is the right choice for you, congratulations! You are going to love every minute you spend with your Great Dane. As you and your new dog get to know each other, you may find that you need to reference key pieces of information from this book. Rather than flipping through the entire thing, in this chapter you will find a Great Dane care sheet which includes all of the most relevant facts about the breed and its care.

1.) Basic Breed Information

Pedigree: bred from large boarhounds originating in Greece, developed in Germany during the 16th century, possibly crossed with English Mastiff and Irish Wolfhound

Breed Size: giant

Height (male): minimum 30 inches (76 cm)

Height (female): minimum 28 inches (71 cm)

Weight (male): minimum 120 lbs. (54 kg)

Weight (female): minimum 100 lbs. (45 kg)

Coat Length: short and close-lying

Coat Texture: smooth and dense

Color: fawn, brindle, blue, black, harlequin, and mantle

Markings: depends on color; may exhibit black mask, tiger-stripe pattern, black patches, or a solid black blanket

Eyes and Nose: dark, matches coat color

Ears: large and triangular, naturally floppy but sometimes cropped to a point

Tail: long and tapered to a point, carried high

Temperament: moderate energy, friendly, affectionate with family, gentle, not aggressive

Training: intelligent and eager to please, easy to housetrain

Exercise Needs: moderately high; 30 minute daily walk is generally sufficient

Lifespan: average 7 to 10 years

Health Conditions: hip dysplasia, gastric torsion, bone cancer, heart disease, developmental issues

2.) Habitat Requirements

Indoor/Outdoor: indoor only

Recommended Accessories: crate, dog bed, food/water dishes, toys, collar, leash, harness, grooming supplies

Collar and Leash: sized by weight

Grooming Supplies: rubber curry comb, gentle dog-friendly shampoo, dog nail clippers,

Grooming Frequency: brush several times a week; professional grooming every 6 months

Exercise Requirements: daily walk plus playtime

Crate: highly recommended

Crate Size: just large enough for dog to lie down and turn around comfortably

Crate Extras: lined with blanket or plush pet bed

Food/Water: stainless steel bowls, clean daily

Toys: start with an assortment, see what the dog likes; include some mentally stimulating toys

3.) Nutritional Information

Nutritional Needs: water, protein, carbohydrate, fats, vitamins, minerals

RER: 30 x (weight in kg) + 70

Calorie Needs: varies by age, weight, and activity level; RER modified with activity level

Amount to Feed (puppy): feed freely but consult recommendations on the package

Amount to Feed (adult): consult recommendations on the package; calculated by weight

Important Ingredients: fresh animal protein (fresh meat, meat meals, eggs), digestible carbohydrates (brown rice, oats, sweet potato), animal fats (chicken fat, salmon oil)

Important Minerals: calcium, phosphorus, potassium, magnesium, iron, copper and manganese

Important Vitamins: Vitamin A, Vitamin B-12, Vitamin D, Vitamin C

Look For: protein at top of ingredients list; digestible carbohydrates; animal fats; no artificial flavors, dyes, or preservatives

4.) Breeding Information

Age of First Heat: around 18 to 24 months

Breeding Age: about 1 year for males, 2 years for females

Heat (Estrus) Cycle: about 2 to 3 weeks

Frequency: twice a year, every 6 to 7 months

Greatest Fertility: 11 to 15 days into the cycle

Gestation Period: 59 to 63 days, about 9 weeks

Pregnancy Detection: possible after 21 days, best to wait 28 days before veterinary examination

Feeding Pregnant Dogs: maintain normal diet until week 4 or 5 then slightly increase rations

Signs of Labor: body temperature drops below normal 100° to 102°F (37.7° to 38.8°C), may be as low as 98°F (36.6°C); dog begins nesting in a dark, quiet place

Contractions: period of 10 minutes in waves of 3 to 5 followed by a period of rest

Whelping: puppies are born in 1/2 hour increments following 10 to 30 minutes of forceful straining

Puppies: born with eyes and ears closed; eyes open at 3 weeks, teeth develop at 10 weeks

Litter Size: average 6 to 8 puppies, up to 16 possible

Weaning: start offering puppy food soaked in water at 4 to 6 weeks; fully weaned by 8 weeks

Socialization: start as early as possible to prevent puppies from being nervous as an adult

Chapter Fourteen: Relevant Websites

   In reading this book you have received a wealth of
information about Great Danes including basic facts and
detailed tips regarding the care for this breed. Even if you
read this book cover to cover, however, you might still have
questions about preparing to become a Great Dane owner.
In this chapter you will find a collection of relevant
websites and useful resources to help answer those
questions. In the following pages you will receive lists of
helpful websites for Great Dane food, crates, beds, toys,
accessories, and general dog care information.

1.) Food for Great Danes

United States Links:

Orijen Large-Breed Puppy Food.

<http://www.orijen.ca/products/dog-food/dry-dog-food/puppy-large/>

Blue Buffalo Large Breed Food and Treats.

<http://bluebuffalo.com/product-finder/dog/large-breed-dog-food-recipes/>

Wellness Complete Health Large Breed Adult Food.

<http://www.wellnesspetfood.com/product-details.aspx?pet=dog&pid=61&dm=completehealth>

Nutro Large Breed Adult Dog Food.

<http://www.nutro.com/natural-dog-food/nutro/dry/large-breed-adult-chicken-whole-brown-rice-oatmeal-recipe.aspx>

"Feeding Large Breed Puppies." Integrative Veterinary Care. <http://ivcjournal.com/feeding-large-breed-puppies/

United Kingdom Links:

Large Breed Dog Food. PetPlanet.co.uk.

<http://www.petplanet.co.uk/category.asp?dept_id=378>

Burns Large Breed Chicken & Brown Rice Food.

<http://burnspet.co.uk/products/burns-for-dogs/large-breed-chicken-brown-rice.html

Canagan Large-Breed Dog Grain-Free Food.

<https://www.canagan.co.uk/large-breed.html>

Acana Large Breed Dog Food.

<http://www.acanapetfoods.co.uk/acatalog/Large_Breed_Dog_Food.html>

"Breed & Size Specific Dog Nutrition." The Kennel Club.

<http://www.thekennelclub.org.uk/getting-a-dog-or-puppy/general-advice-about-caring-for-your-new-puppy-or-dog/feeding-your-puppy-or-dog/breed-and-size-specific-dog-nutrition/>

2.) Crates and Beds for Great Danes

United States Links:

Dog Beds and Mats. In the Company of Dogs.

<http://www.inthecompanyofdogs.com/ShopCategory.aspx
?ID=17,470>

Dog Beds, Crates & Gear. Chewy.com.

<http://www.chewy.com/dog/crates-kennels-369>

Dog Beds. Wayfair.com.

<http://www.wayfair.com/Dog-Beds-C409475.html>

Crates, Carriers and Pens. Doctors Foster and Smith.

<http://www.drsfostersmith.com/dog-supplies/dog-cages-
crates-carriers-pens/ps/c/3307/10627>

Crates, Gates & Containment. PetSmart.com.

<http://www.petsmart.com/dog/crates-gates-containment/
cat-36-catid-100013>

United Kingdom Links:

Dog Beds and Bedding. Pet-Supermarket.co.uk.

<http://www.pet-supermarket.co.uk/Category/Dog_Supplies-Dog_Beds_Bedding>

Dog Crates. PetPlanet.co.uk.

<http://www.petplanet.co.uk/category.asp?dept_id=771>

Dog Beds and Baskets. ZooPlus.co.uk.

<http://www.zooplus.co.uk/shop/dogs/dog_beds_baskets>

Dog Crates & Dog Cages. CroftOnline.co.uk.

<http://www.croftonline.co.uk/dog-crates-and-cages.html>

"The 10 Best Dog Beds." Independent.co.uk.

<http://www.independent.co.uk/property/interiors/the-10-best-dog-beds-8775162.html>

Dog Crates & Dog Travel. ZooPlus.co.uk.

<http://www.zooplus.co.uk/shop/dogs/dog_cages_carriers>

3.) Toys and Accessories for Great Danes

United States Links:

Collars, Harnesses & Leashes. Petco.

<http://www.petco.com/N_22_4294956566/Dog-Collars-Harnesses-and-Leashes.aspx>

Dog Bowls and Feeders. Chewy.com.

<http://www.chewy.com/dog/bowls-feeders-338>

Dog Toys. Pet Mountain.

<http://www.petmountain.com/category/33/1/dog-toys.html>

Dog Grooming Supplies. PetSmart.

<http://www.petsmart.com/dog/grooming-supplies/cat-36-catid-100016>

"Dog Toys; How to Pick the Best and Safest." Humane Society. <http://www.humanesociety.org/animals/dogs/tips/dog_toys.html?referrer=https://www.google.com/>

United Kingdom Links:

Dog Toys. Fetch.co.uk.

<https://fetch.co.uk/dogs/dog-toys>

Dog Supplies and Dog Toys. Pet-Supermarket.co.uk.

<http://www.pet-supermarket.co.uk/Category/Dog_
Supplies-Dog_Toys>

Dog Collars and Leads. Pets at Home.

<http://www.petsathome.com/shop/en/pets/dog/dog-
collars-and-leads

Dog Bowls and Feeders. PetPlanet.co.uk.

<http://www.petplanet.co.uk/category.asp?dept_id=528>

Dog Grooming Equipment. Simpsons-Online.co.uk.

<http://simpsons-online.co.uk/dog-grooming/equipment/>

"The 10 Best Dog Collars." Independent.co.uk.

<http://www.independent.co.uk/extras/indybest/outdoor-
activity/best-dog-collars-10437828.html>

4.) General Dog Care Information

United States Links:

"Ten Dog Care Essentials." Humane Society.
<http://www.humanesociety.org/animals/dogs/tips/dog_car e_essentials.html>

"Principles of Dog Nutrition." PetMD.
<http://www.petmd.com/dog/nutrition/evr_dg_principles_ of_dog_nutrition>

"Training Your Dog." ASPCA. <https://www.aspca. org/pet-care/virtual-pet-behaviorist/dog-behavior/training- your-dog>

Pet Care Center: Dog. PetMD.
<http://www.petmd.com/dog/petcare>

"Breeding Your Dog." K9Web.com.
<http://www.k9web.com/dog-faqs/breeding.html>

Dog Symptoms and Conditions A to Z. WebMD.
<http://pets.webmd.com/dogs/symptoms/>

United Kingdom Links:

Dogs – Dog Welfare, Tips, Advice, Health. RSPCA.
<http://www.rspca.org.uk/adviceandwelfare/pets/dogs>

Nutritional Guidelines for Dogs. FEDIAF.
<http://www.ethical-pets.co.uk/blog/wp-
content/uploads/2012/10/FEDIAF_Nutritional_Guidelines_-
_final_version_6-09-11.pdf>

Online Encyclopedia of Common Dog Health Problems.
<http://www.mans-best-friend.org.uk/canine-health-online-
encyclopedia.htm>

Puppy and Dog Training Tips. APDT.co.uk.
<http://www.apdt.co.uk/dog-owners/puppy-dog-training-
tips>

"Breeding Your Dog." The Kennel Club.
<http://www.thekennelclub.org.uk/breeding/breeding-
from-your-dog/

"Dog Tips." Association of Pet Behavior Counsellors.
<http://www.apbc.org.uk/tips/dog>

Index

C

G

H

Q

R

S

T

Photo Credits

Cover Page Photo By Flickr user NJClicks,
<https://www.flickr.com/photos/njcav/6467358141/sizes/l>

Page 1 Photo By Fainomenon via Wikimedia Commons,
<https://en.wikipedia.org/wiki/Great_Dane#/
media/File:Duffy_the_brindle_Great_Dane.JPG>

Page 8 Photo By Kris Kasawski via Wikimedia Commons,
<https://commons.wikimedia.org/wiki/File:Black_Great_Da
ne.jpg>

Page 11 Photo By Flickr user MapHobbit,
<https://www.flickr.com/photos/trazomfreak/3033307686/si
zes/o/>

Page 17 Photo By Johan Christof Merck via Wikimedia
Commons, <https://en.wikipedia.org/wiki/Great_Dane#/
media/File:Johann_Christof_Merck_-_Ulmer_Dogge_-
_WGA15061.jpg>

Page 20 Photo By Flickr user Robstephaustralia, <https://www.flickr.com/photos/robandstephanielevy/2657327293/sizes/l>

Page 21 Photo By Flickr user Laertes, <https://www.flickr.com/photos/jonhurd/553947012/sizes/l>

Page 22 Photo By Jon Hurd via Wikimedia Commons, https://en.wikipedia.org/wiki/File:Stella_of_the_Dunes.jpg>

Page 25 Photo By Flickr user Laertes, <https://www.flickr.com/photos/jonhurd/3561645042/sizes/l>

Page 38 Photo By Pixabay User 825545, <https://pixabay.com/en/great-dane-grey-tiger-small-hybrid-662814/>

Page 46 Photo By Flickr user Laertes, <https://www.flickr.com/photos/jonhurd/2511652978/sizes/l>

Page 53 Photo By Viborg via Wikimedia Commons, <https://en.wikipedia.org/wiki/File:Dogge_Odin.jpg>

Page 59 Photo By Flickr user Jwillier2,
<https://www.flickr.com/photos/jwillier/3906964747/sizes/l>

Page 71 Photo By India Lipton via Wikimedia Commons,
<https://commons.wikimedia.org/wiki/File:Great_Dane_Blu
e_Charlton_Wiki_7Months.jpg>

Page 81 Photo By Gotdanes via Wikimedia Commons,
<https://commons.wikimedia.org/wiki/File:Fawnequin.jpg>

Page 86 Photo By Jon Hurd via Wikimedia Commons,
<https://commons.wikimedia.org/wiki/File:Great_Danes_ha
rlequin_and_fawn.jpg>

Page 89 Photo By Marta Picztarska via Wikimedia
Commons, <https://commons.wikimedia.org/wiki/
File:Dog_niemiecki_6_tygodni-_Great_Dane_-
_6_weeks_puppy_(2176102845).jpg>

Page 95 Photo By Fainomenon via Wikimedia Commons,
<https://en.wikipedia.org/wiki/File:Gt._Dane,_Lucy.JPG>

Page 106 Photo By Flickr user Docoverachiever, <https://www.flickr.com/photos/sheila_sund/8256611536/sizes/l>

Page 114 Photo By DeviantArt user xxtgxxstock, <http://xxtgxxstock.deviantart.com/art/Great-Dane-21-460016436>

Page 120 Photo By Pixabay user BelaMarie, <https://pixabay.com/en/dog-great-dane-harlequin-blue-eyes-749191/>

Page 125 Photo By Melissa via Wikimedia Commons, <https://en.wikipedia.org/wiki/File:Great_Dane_black_laying.jpg>

Page 132 Photo By Sachin Patekar via PD Pics, <http://www.pdpics.com/photo/3164-dog-breeds-great-dane/>

References

"Breeding: Pregnancy and Puppy Viability."
Cynologist.com. <http://cynologist.com/index.php/
anatomy-of-dog/breeding-pregnancy-and-puppy-
viability>

"Dog Nutrition Tips." ASPCA.
<https://www.aspca.org/pet-care/dog-care/dog-
nutrition-tips>

"Dog Show Training Tips and Techniques for Beginners."
Udemy Blog. <https://blog.udemy.com/dog-show-
training/>

"Estrus Cycle in Dogs." VCA Animal Hospitals.
<http://www.vcahospitals.com/main/pet-health-
information/article/animal-health/estrus-cycles-in-
dogs/5778>

"Great Dane." Dog Breed Information Center.
<http://www.dogbreedinfo.com/greatdane.htm>

"Great Dane." Dogtime.com. <http://dogtime.com/dog-
breeds/great-dane>

"Great Danes." Embrace Pet Insurance.
<http://www.embracepetinsurance.com/dog-
breeds/great-dane>

"Great Dane Breed Information." VetStreet.
<http://www.vetstreet.com/dogs/great-dane>

"Great Dane Colors, Coat Patterns & Markings." All About
Great Danes. <http://www.all-about-great-
danes.com/great-dane-colors.html>

"Great Dane FAQ: Frequently Asked Questions About Great Dane Dogs." Your Purebred Puppy. <http://www.yourpurebredpuppy.com/faq/greatdanes.html>

"Great Dane Guide." Animal Planet. <http://www.animalplanet.com/breed-selector/dog-breeds/working/great-dane.html>

"Great Dane History." AKC.org. <http://www.akc.org/dog-breeds/great-dane/detail/#history>

"Grooming a Great Dane." All-About-Great-Danes. <http://www.all-about-great-danes.com/grooming-a-great-dane.html>

"How Much do Great Danes Cost?" Here Pup! <http://herepup.com/how-much-do-great-danes-cost/>

"How to Choose a Healthy Puppy." Pet Education. <http://www.peteducation.com/article.cfm?c=2+2106&aid=841>

"How to Find a Responsible Dog Breeder." The Humane Society. <http://www.humanesociety.org/issues/puppy_mills/tips/finding_responsible_dog_breeder.html?referrer=https://www.google.com/>

"Licensing and Registration Under the Animal Welfare Act." APHIS. <https://www.aphis.usda.gov/animal_welfare/downloads/aw/awlicreg.pdf>

"Nutrition – General Feeding Guidelines for Dogs." VCA Animal Hospitals. <http://www.vcahospitals.com/main/pet-health-information/article/animal-health/nutrition-general-feeding-guidelines-for-dogs/6491>

"Official Standard for the Great Dane." Great Dane Club of America. <http://www.gdca.org/great-dane-standard.html>

"Official Standard of the Great Dane." AKC.org. <http://cdn.akc.org/GreatDane.pdf>

"Purchasing a Great Dane." Great Dane Club of America. <http://www.gdca.org/purchasing-a-great-dane.html>

"So You're Thinking About Getting a Great Dane?" Toddborg.com. <http://toddborg.com/danes.htm>

"The Estimated Cost of Adopting a Great Dane." California Dreaming Great Danes. <http://californiadreaminggreatdanes.com/costofpup.html>

"Think You Want a Dane?" Dames for Danes Great Dane Rescue. <http://www.damesfordanes.org/Think_you_want_a_Dane_.html>

"Training Great Danes." Your Purebred Puppy. <http://www.yourpurebredpuppy.com/training/greatdanes.html>

"Training Great Danes, Socialization, Behavior, Conditioning, Tips, Tricks, & Techniques. How & Why." All-About-GreatDanes. <http://www.all-about-great-danes.com/training-great-danes.html>

CPSIA information can be obtained
at www.ICGtesting.com
Printed in the USA
BVOW07s2304171116
468204BV00004BA/47/P